T0381100

BREAKING
the CHAINS *of*
RELIGIOUS ILLUSION

CHRISTINE PETERS

BALBOA.PRESS
A DIVISION OF HAY HOUSE

Balboa Press books may be ordered through booksellers or by contacting:

Balboa Press
A Division of Hay House
1663 Liberty Drive
Bloomington, IN 47403
www.balboapress.com
844-682-1282

Print information available on the last page.

Scripture quotations are taken from the Holy Bible, King James Version.

ISBN: 979-8-7652-4974-1 (sc)
ISBN: 979-8-7652-4975-8 (hc)
ISBN: 979-8-7652-4973-4 (e)

Library of Congress Control Number: 2024903173

Balboa Press rev. date: 05/08/2024

I dedicate this book to my inner child.
You are heard and I acknowledge you.
I love you sweet, precious child.

CONTENTS

PREFACE

I believe in God, a higher power, the Creator of All That Is, the powerful entity of the universe. I do believe there is something much greater than us, guiding our lives and enabling us to have free will, love, and light in our lives. There are many religions in this world. Some I understand; others, not so much. All the teachings of all the different belief systems seem to have one thing in common, and that thing is a *mighty higher power*. In my mind, I finally figured out that no matter what one calls this higher power—God, Jesus, Buddha, Jehovah, etc.—these titles are all names for the same higher power. It's kind of like this higher power has many nicknames.

I'd like to think that this higher power has a real unique sense of humor. When I look around me, I see so many things that we, as human beings, get ourselves into unwittingly, and then we pray, asking God to "help us" as we try to figure out how to help ourselves without losing face.

Now, I wasn't always this open-minded, and some may say, "That Christine gal is crazy!" Maybe they are right. But at this stage in my life, I have come to realize that religion is totally different from "being spiritual."

Many people seem to think that being "spiritual" is not a surefire way to get to heaven. Many people seem to feel that you can only go to heaven if you repent, be baptized, speak in tongues, or "accept Jesus into your heart, and you'll be saved." I've seen and heard many different opinions about being saved, and I now realize that everything I was taught from a very young age was all just man-made rules according to how a preacher or anyone in authority over me (as a child) chose to interpret the scripture, as written "by men."

This book is about my personal journey of healing from spiritual abuse along with emotional, physical, and sexual abuse, all brought about by being a member of a religious cult at a very early age. This is not a book for the faint of heart. Some of the things written here are raw with emotion and are my life story, which shaped and molded me into the person I am today. If I can help one person by writing this book, I will die happy and fulfilled. So buckle your seatbelt and take this journey with me toward healing a broken spirit and mind. I promise there will be laughter and tears as some of the journeys written on these pages might jog your memories about your own that you need to heal from. Together, we can make a difference for future generations if we just step out of the box we have all been taught to believe in and allow ourselves to ask questions about what we believe.

Let us begin.

CHAPTER 1
CHILDHOOD AND RECOGNIZING RELIGION

I was born a sensitive child. I have always been able to feel other people's feelings, even with no verbal communication. I am told by relatives that I was a very quiet child; I didn't cry much but watched everything going on around me with big eyes. I was always looking around and feeling all the emotions around me.

I felt fear for the first time as a toddler standing in the sun as it cast a shadow on the wall in our front room by the door. I was playing with how the shadow moved on the wall, and suddenly, I thought I saw the shadow move in a way that I had not moved. It scared me, and I immediately moved away and never played with my shadow again.

My next memory was when my family moved to Elk City, Oklahoma. It was a long drive through the desert, where there were small patches of vegetation with sand, cacti, and dust in every direction. I thought it was beautiful and was in awe of the lush green grass in the middle of all the heat of the desert. I was only three or so when we arrived in Oklahoma.

We settled in as a family, and soon enough, I began kindergarten. I was very shy and struggled with walking to school as the path led right through the junior and high school grounds, and many mornings, the high schoolers would try to pick on me and tweak my dress up as I passed through. I hated the attention and would usually run so as not to provide them with a chance to bother me. I was afraid and didn't know how to stand up for myself. My mother had to walk with me a few times before the big kids finally left me alone. She never said a word to them. Her look said it all: leave my daughter alone. I was finally able to walk to school in peace, for a while at least. I came away from that experience with the realization that, somehow, I was different; and for whatever reason, it made people want to pick on me. It never occurred to me that, perhaps, I was cute and easy prey because of my personality and looks. I just remember hating the attention and humiliation of these people who were bigger than I was.

The town we lived in was rather small. There was only one school, which had all twelve grades; but there were separate buildings that housed grade school students, junior high students, and high schoolers. Once I reached grade school, there were music classes and holiday parties for Halloween and Christmas. I became aware that I wasn't allowed to participate in these activities as they were "against our religion." I didn't fully understand why I couldn't participate. I just knew I would find myself in a great deal of trouble with my parents and God if I didn't sit in the hall away from the festivities. I was being taught that having a Christmas tree was like worshipping a graven image and should be avoided. "Thou shalt not worship graven images" is one of the Ten Commandments, and I was being taught to follow the Ten Commandments.

By the time I entered second grade, I realized I was very different from the other kids. I dressed differently, my hair was different, and I was taught that participating in "pagan" activities would send me straight to hell. Therefore, we celebrated no holidays such as Christmas, Halloween, our birthdays, Valentine's Day, or anything else deemed pagan by the pastor of the church we attended. At such a tender age, I never questioned why I had to obey all these rules. My thought was that all the kids around me just didn't know any better, and I felt sorry for them because I just knew they were all destined for hell for not obeying the Bible. I thought God was surely frowning down on these children whom I attended school with every day. I was too scared of my parents and God to ever question anything I was told.

CHRISTINE PETERS

Needless to say, I confess that school was not my favorite place to be. I would play sick sometimes to avoid going, but my mom caught on to what I was doing and stopped it immediately! Oh well, that was my way of rebelling at the time!

Life seemed full, and there was always something to do. My sister and I would go to school, come home to do our chores, and attend church. A lot. Church services were held three times a week, and in between services, there were social activities organized by the ladies of the church. These functions included anything from baby showers to Bible studies, and often, the ladies would gather to make peanut brittle or baked goods. The ladies were always looking for ways to make money for the church fund, but the socialization with church members also kept one from straying out into the world and being friends with anyone "not of the church." These outsiders were sinners and not to be trusted.

About the time I turned seven, a new preacher came to town. He wanted to start a new church and was all fired up about the "path to salvation." My parents decided to invite the preacher and his wife to our house for dinner. Back in those days, children were taught to be seen but not heard. My sister and I worked with Mom all day, doing extra cleaning and making sure everything was sparkling clean for this special guest and his wife. A small card table was set up for us children, as we were not allowed to eat at the big table with the grown-ups, but we were allowed to be in the same room. Mom introduced my sister and me to the preacher. I looked up at him, and I distinctly remember his eyes. There was something about his eyes that made me immediately feel fearful. It was like looking into a deep pit of black ink that was so thick one couldn't see through it to feel any light. He was quite tall, and I remember feeling overwhelmed by his size.

When he took my hand, he didn't try to be gentle as he shook it. Instead, his grip was strong, painful, and powerful. I felt a cold sensation of fear slide down my back. It felt awful, evil, and unclean to me; although, at the time, I was too young to know the right words to communicate this feeling. I recall after they ate and left, I went to my mom and said, "I don't like that preacher, Mama!"

My mother slapped me, scolded me, and told me not to talk about a man of God that way ever again. I learned right then to keep my mouth shut and not speak out loud or voice my true feelings, for there would be punishment for sure.

Shortly thereafter, this preacher and his wife moved to our town and began their church, of which my family became members. As I said earlier, Elk City was a pretty small town. It was the kind of town where everybody knew everybody, and they always tried to help one another out when possible. My dad had started his own plumbing business, and it was doing well. He was well-known and liked around town and had a good reputation for quality work. I was my dad's little shadow! He had infinite patience with me and answered any questions I threw his way. I became a real tomboy in my long dresses and sleeves. My mother was often aggravated with how dirty I would get crawling around under houses with Dad. If there was one thing anyone who met me agreed on, it was that I was a "daddy's girl." Oh, how I loved my dad! He nicknamed me Pooh, and if Dad was home, I was hanging on his shirttail. I have many happy memories of spending time with my dad.

On Saturday mornings, he would take me with him on his plumbing calls; but before the first appointment, he would stop at the local Daylight Donuts, let me pick any donut I wanted, and allow me to have a cup of coffee to go with it (with cream and sugar). These outings always made me feel so special because he allowed me to choose what I wanted. You see, until this point in my life, I had very few choices about things like my hair, my clothing, or my shoes. Everything was regulated by the rules of the church, so getting to choose a simple donut was really special. My mom was pretty strict about wearing certain types of clothes, staying clean, and having good manners. It was a sin to not abide by the rules of society and the church about how to dress and how to have good manners—I could go on, but you understand my meaning.

I adored my dad. He gave me the opportunity to just be a kid during those times when it was just him and me. Dad didn't criticize me, preach at me, or judge me and tell me I was going to hell. I received enough of that at church from the preacher. Dad didn't care if I got dirt on my dress or hands. I remember him telling me, "Now, Pooh, let's keep our trip for a donut to ourselves 'cause you know your mom wouldn't like us eating all this sugar!" So I kept my mouth shut. I could climb trees and go fishing with Dad; or sometimes, during the hot long summers, I would hike up my long skirt and go wading in a cool creek. It didn't matter to Dad that my ankles might show. I was just a little kid trying to have a few moments of joy!

Sometimes Dad would work on the weekends at an old house the members of the church bought with the intention of converting it into a real church building. The irony of this is as I got older and looked back, this very building my beloved dad was working on would be the place where my worst nightmare would occur. He was quite handy with all aspects of remodeling and always wanted to help the church family. I always went where Dad was. I felt safe with my dad. I knew he would always protect me. Many times, I would grow tired, curl up, and go to sleep in a corner until Dad would pick me up and carry me to our van for the drive home.

Once this house was bought to turn into a church, the ladies of the congregation stepped up with more ideas for money-making schemes so there would be funds for the renovations needed: peanut brittle, baked goods, donuts, and anything they could think of to make and sell. The children would be sent out door-to-door, selling these goods house-to-house. The children were used for this because it was harder for people to say no to a child than an adult. So every Saturday, I was selling either donuts or peanut brittle and being expected to "witness and invite" total strangers to come to church. This always made me feel very uncomfortable, but it became a way of life. It didn't matter if you were sick or didn't want to go. This had to be done to further the "God cause" and "build the church." To this day, I still cannot stand peanut brittle!

The church ladies even organized a fifteen-mile walkathon, and children, as well as adults, participated. We walked along the highway for the whole fifteen-mile trek. It was hot, and I was tired, but I made it. The next day, my parents were so exhausted from the blisters that formed on their feet they could hardly get out of bed. I didn't have blisters, but I was glad to be home. We sure did make a decent amount of money for that church fund.

The Church

Within a few months, the new church building was pretty much done. The first service was a large celebration, which turned into a full-blown revival. There was a guest evangelist who fired up everyone about going to hell. It motivated us to reexamine our lives to ensure we were on the right path to heaven. We needed to go out, witness, and bring people into the flock to save their souls. We were taught, as good Christians, that it was our duty to tell all the lost souls around us about a better path to God and heaven. The scripture we used the most was Acts 2:38 (KJV): "Repent, and be baptized every one of you in the name of Jesus Christ for the remission of sins, and ye shall receive the gift of the Holy Ghost." Then we would explain the Holy Ghost with more scripture from the Bible. This was considered part of the salvation of our souls. God required these duties from us, the chosen people, so we preached. We were taught that God would be unhappy with us if we did not witness. By not witnessing, we were hiding our faith and beliefs, which was not how God expected us to live.

Many of the people in our town began hearing about this new church and were leery about it. The townsfolk talked about how the people in our congregation were shouting and dancing in the spirit and speaking in tongues. I can recall many times I had a door shut in my face when I would go out to witness door-to-door in random neighborhoods. People had no desire to hear about our faith. It was considered odd and unusual.

The evangelist preaching the revival had his own ideas about salvation and how best to serve God. The following is a list of things one had to give up to be pleasing in the eyes of the Lord:

- holidays, including birthdays or government holidays
- modern clothes; the dress code to follow involved long skirts, long sleeves, high neckline, no pants or shorts or swimwear
- makeup
- haircut (women could not cut their hair) or use rubber bands as they might cut the hair off when styling
- pieces of jewelry

- pictures on walls
- toys that could be mistaken for a graven image (no dolls, stuffed animals, Barbies, etc.)
- mixed swimming and bathing suits (Your body must be covered at all times.)
- music except for gospel music
- TV
- medical doctors (no vaccines)
- competitions (sports or board games)

Now that I was turning eight years old and better able to understand, I felt the burden of these rules. I was beginning to feel a fear about doing anything that might send me to hell.

I recall feeling so pouty, angry, and sad the day my parents had a big yard sale and sold all the things deemed "sinful." I recall my mom telling me to adjust my attitude as God wouldn't be happy with a girl who has a poor attitude. I went inside to a quiet corner and cried. I didn't understand why God wouldn't be happy with me; but I quickly figured out that if I didn't do what I was told, God would "get me" somehow, and it wouldn't be good. I was still pretty young, and all the preaching I was exposed to filled my mind with fearful consequences for anything deemed bad in the eyes of the Lord. Children are such sponges. They are vulnerable, and all these rules and fearful teachings were sticking in my brain more solidly with each passing day. These teachings were embedding a foundation of fear within my very core. My soul and I had no idea just how much these ideas would shape my life as I grew older.

Life was beginning to be a never-ending revival, or so it seemed to me. There was always another revival, and the services seemed to last longer and longer late into the night. It wasn't unusual for the church to let out well past eleven o'clock at night. These revivals would last two and three weeks at a time, and usually, the speakers were from out of town, just traveling through our area. I became attached to a couple of these evangelists as they came around several times a year. One was a little Mexican gentleman. He would get so excited and run all over the stage while shouting out his sermon. He would wave a white handkerchief above his head, spinning it around and around quickly as "the spirit" would move him to preach. He was full of good-natured humor and seemed to have a soft spot for children. I found his style of sermon refreshing as he would use humor to soften the blow of hellfire and brimstone. This man could sing like an angel! He sang several songs designed to give messages about what one must do to get to heaven. I remember him being quite pleasant to visit with, and he was always nice to me.

Another evangelist who came frequently was a man with five children in his family. Three of his children were girls, who were all in their teenage years. They were a ragtag family, and it was obvious they didn't have much. We would go through our closets and give them clothes to wear when they came through town. One of these girls, my favorite, taught me how to play piano by ear during one of the visits. We would beg our mother to allow them to stay the night with us. We were so attached to them. These girls were so sweet but also very fearful of their father, who was extremely strict with them in their appearances and manners. These girls were not allowed to wear deodorant or shave their underarms or legs. They were very self-conscious of their bodies. Still, we had many good times playing piano together and always missed them when they left.

During one such revival, the evangelist decided that everyone should pray one hour a day. So before we would start our day each morning, Mom would wake us while it was still dark, and we would all go into the front room and pray for one hour. I would ask God to bless everyone I could think of, but I had a short list. My family members, of course, and the church people. I couldn't help myself. I would get so sleepy that I would fall asleep while kneeling in the recliner, and Dad would gently shake me awake before anybody else noticed that I was sleeping instead of praying. I wish I could tell you that I became really good at praying for a solid hour without falling asleep, but alas, that never happened. I always ran out of things to pray about far before the hour was up, so I always fell asleep. I finally reached a point where I just couldn't remember any more names, and I figured that if God was big and fearful enough to punish me, then perhaps he could remember all the people I was supposed to pray for and bless them without me having to list each name aloud into the heavens. He is God, after all. We were being taught that God even knew how many hairs were on my head, so surely, He would also know all the people I meant to pray for without me having to say all of them by name. I don't know what everybody else was praying about, but apparently, whatever the preacher was praying about went unanswered to his satisfaction. The next thing I knew, he said we had to fast along with our prayer.

As a seven-year-old child, the fasting process can be pretty tough. We were often fasting three to seven days at a time. Grown-ups and children alike. Nothing but water. Period. I was so hungry, but at the same time, I was too scared to eat for fear of punishment. This fasting was supposed to humble us and make us more obedient and faithful. It was supposed to help us stay focused on God. I can't say it helped my focus much being a young child. I remember how hungry I was and how hard it was to drink only water when the hunger pangs were so bad in my belly. I tried desperately to stay prayerful and think about God, but I struggled. I have no memories of how I dealt with fasting in school. Try as I might, I just don't recall dealing with this around my classmates and teachers. I do remember going to the grocery store with my mother during one of these fasts. It was the last day of a seven-day fast, and Mom was stocking up to cook a good meal. We were walking through the produce department, and I remember how wonderful the green grapes looked. My mouth began watering. I wanted to reach out and pluck a grape so desperately from the cluster lying there in front of me. To this day, I have a dislike for grocery shopping as it brings back bad memories for me.

Somehow, I learned to turn the hunger feelings off to get through and, in doing so, ended up with an eating disorder in my twenties, which I had to deal with through counseling and medication in my adult years. I learned, with professional help, that most eating disorders are about control. It's about controlling ourselves or our environment. For me, I simply learned how to control the hunger pangs to the point that the gland in my brain had stopped producing the chemical that tells us it's time to eat. I literally never felt any hunger for years on up to adulthood. This was how I coped as a child to endure the fasting of the church.

Once I reached adulthood, I had no idea just how little I ate. I confess I just didn't pay attention to my body. I had been taught in my early years to only concentrate on God and my faith, to only think about being good enough to get to heaven, and to witness to people by example how I lived my life. Thinking about my body was only considered when it came to how I dressed and cleanliness. For years, it never occurred to me to think about what my body might need to stay healthy and balanced.

Then, once counseling began, I reached a point where I was struggling to eat anything solid. As I began dealing with all my hidden issues, I felt I was in total control of my life. When I began feeling as if I was losing control, I didn't want to eat. I had no idea I was depriving myself of nutrition. I finally reached a point where I was not able to ignore the food issue any longer. When I realized I was drinking Ensure and eating no solid food, I made myself a doctor's appointment to confront why I wasn't eating solid food.

Thankfully, the internist I saw was very kind to me. I told him I needed to be able to eat. I was worried about myself because I realized I was only drinking Ensure. I cried that day and told him I didn't understand how I had gotten to this point in my life. I was thirty-four years old and only weighed eighty-eight pounds. I had finally really taken a good look at myself in the mirror and was shocked at what I saw. I confessed to him that I was seeing a counselor and had discovered my life was so very full of issues I didn't even know I had, and I was working on them. He offered me some medication and set me up with an eating disorder specialist, who was very helpful. Within a few months, the worst was over. I was able to eat solid food again, and it's been a steady climb back up for me to maintain my weight.

I took the medication for about six months, and finally, I began to feel hunger pangs. I remember feeling so amazed the first time I recognized I felt hungry. It was the most amazing feeling! I was in awe of my own body. The counselor I saw helped me discover that my eating issue stemmed from all the fasting done as a child. My body had to be kick-started to remember how to feel hungry again. The counseling and medication worked! I had healed one of my issues. I was making progress in my mental health and beginning to bring my life back into a healthier balance.

CHRISTINE PETERS

THE DEVIL'S GONNA GET YOU

There was a lady who started coming to church. The first time I saw her, I remember thinking she was so beautiful! She had thick long mahogany-red hair and spoke so softly. She was tall for a lady and slender and carried herself so elegantly. I admired her long hair. It was hanging down past her knees! I was envious of her beautiful hair. My hair was fine and mousy, and it just didn't seem to grow very much. I believe she had been through a recent divorce and just wanted to be part of a family of people who looked after one another. My sister and I spent many Sunday afternoons visiting with her. She seemed to enjoy being around children, and it was common for the church people to go home with one another in between services on Sundays.

It was always enjoyable to spend a Sunday afternoon with Bessie. It was on one of these afternoons that my sister and I noticed that Bessie was a bit off. She just wasn't her usual self. She had a hard time sitting down and seemed to pace and prowl around her home during our visit.

As church time got closer, she seemed to calm down. We went to the car and got in to head to Sunday night services. The service began as it usually did with prayer requests and announcements. Bessie stood up and requested prayers for herself. The preacher asked her to come forward to the front of the church so he could anoint her with olive oil and "lay hands" on her at the altar. We all bowed our heads and began to pray for Bessie. Once the prayer was done, she quietly went back to her seat.

The song director got up and began leading the congregation in song. I was called up to play the piano for the songs. I had taken some piano lessons and could also play by ear, so I would frequently fill in for the other lady who played if she was absent. I always enjoyed the singing part of the service. People would clap along and dance in the aisle, getting all excited as they sang praises to the Lord. Once the song director led five or six songs, it was time for some Bible-thumping, hellfire-and-brimstone preaching, which eventually led to a fired-up altar call. One could run to the altar and cry and repent of their sins.

The preacher sure could get wound up with all that shouting and preaching about what God expected one to do to ensure they go to heaven. He especially seemed to enjoy preaching about how the devil could get into you and steer you in the wrong direction! Never once could I tell you about any preaching about a loving or a forgiving God. It was always about sinning and going to hell for all eternity. I soaked in everything the preacher said about God punishing people for not doing right and following the rules laid down by the good book, and he always had scripture to back up what he was preaching. I believed everything I heard with all my heart and was scared that if I stepped out of line, God would get me! I had already formed my own opinion of a scary, fearful God who punishes people who don't follow the rules. I was beginning to have a real, extreme fear of God, and it had nothing to do with respect at all!

The preacher was beginning to really get into his preaching; all was quiet but the sound of his voice. Suddenly, we all heard mumbling from the back of the room. Bessie had gotten up from the pew and began wandered around. Whatever she was muttering was unintelligible, but it was obvious she was becoming agitated about something. I looked over my shoulder and saw that she was moving her head back and forth like she was having a conversation with herself. She began to get louder and was beginning to disrupt the service, drawing attention away from the preaching.

Now, I know from my own experiences that one should never disturb the preacher while he is preaching. He would call you out and have the deacons escort you to the front of the church to the altar and be prayed over and, if need be, have that misbehaving demon cast out of your body!

This preacher didn't mess around. You better act right or suffer the consequences of your actions! As I watched Bessie, I began to feel a flush of apprehension and fear. Something was very wrong here. She was acting really strange, like nothing I had ever seen before.

All of a sudden, she became silent, so the preacher resumed his sermon. He was beginning to raise his voice more loudly and shout about hell and demons. Bessie suddenly stood up again and once again began muttering and wandering around the back pews. She began spewing profanities toward the preacher and others around her, and her voice kept changing pitch. At times, it sounded almost guttural.

The preacher called for the deacons to escort her to the front of the church to the altar so they could pray over her and release her demons. Surely, the devil was among us this night as somebody in the congregation was being disobedient to God!

I don't mind telling you I was scared! The most scared I had ever been in my whole short life. Nothing had prepared me for what I was seeing and experiencing, much less how this woman was acting. The moment the deacons took hold of her arms, she began fighting them and screeching. Somehow, she stripped her clothes off as they dragged her up the center aisle, screaming horrible profanities all the way! The sounds this woman made were like from a wild animal deep in a jungle, wounded and scared. By the time the deacons got her down to the altar, she had nothing on but her bra and panties and was still fighting them tooth and nail. They wrestled her to the floor and began crying out in prayer to release the devil inside her soul. The tension in the room was so thick you could feel it resting on your skin.

Bessie vomited. The stench of that vomit remains with me even now as I write this. It was so pungent. She suddenly stopped kicking and screaming as the deacons continued to pray over her. The preacher, in the meantime, got the bottle of olive oil and was getting ready to anoint her and cast the demons out. Before he laid his hands on her, he instructed the rest of us to repeat the name of Jesus over and over, or the demons would leave her and come into us if we weren't careful!

I sat in my pew, terrified, saying the name of Jesus over and over for hours, it seemed. I was so scared I was going to be taken over by a horrible demon. One Jesus bled into another—I was saying it so fast! I just knew I didn't want any demon taking over my body. I had enough to worry about trying to follow all the rules now I had one more to worry about—a demon!

I was still sitting in that pew at 1:00 a.m., saying Jesus over and over as the police and paramedics arrived. Poor Bessie was put into a straitjacket and hauled out of the church in an ambulance. No one ever heard or saw Bessie again, and no one ever spoke about that church service again, to my knowledge. I was scared that even though I had done exactly what I was told to do, that stupid demon would get into my body somehow, and I would never be the same. From that moment on, it was a constant battle to make sure I was good enough not to let any evil demon take over how I acted or treated others.

Cultish Behavior

There are many, many different types of cults. In my opinion, all are harmful to the mental, emotional, and spiritual development of an individual and their own built-in system that we call intuition or, to make it simpler, our feelings. Our feelings keep us in check. They are a moral compass to help guide us and know the difference between right and wrong. We are all born with feelings from the moment we make our entrance into this world. This is something that comes naturally to us as humans.

At such a young age of being exposed to unusual religious beliefs, I found that I needed to "turn off" my feelings to survive. I was too young to realize how damaging this would be for me as I got older and tried to navigate the real world and be a productive citizen once I graduated from school.

Amazingly, there can also be some very positive experiences from being in a cult. For example, the opportunity to socialize with other like-minded people can be fun and inspirational. The power of prayers when two or more are gathered together is a good example. (There is a scripture in the King James Version of the Bible that states the above.)

The music and singing were amazing! I have many happy memories of singing with the ladies in the church. Some of these ladies had such beautiful voices. One particular song, "Lily of the Valley," was one of my favorites. They would start singing, and I would go to the piano and, with no written music to follow, peck a few keys and figure out what chords to play. I would follow along and just put my heart into playing a beautiful tune. I enjoyed playing the piano. Depending on the mood I was feeling at the time, I could play softly or pound out my frustrations on those ivory keys without anyone knowing my true feelings.

Music kept me out of trouble and my feelings silent. This kept me from harsh punishment. Anytime I voiced a negative emotion (anger or frustration), I got punished. To be able to let some of those feelings out by playing the piano provided me with a form of healthy release. In a cult atmosphere, one is not allowed to have any negative emotion toward anything. If one had negative emotions, they were told to repent, brought down to the altar to cast out the demons of negativity, or humiliated in front of the entire congregation until they voiced their apology for such sinful, negative thoughts.

There was also a lot of emphasis placed on one's body and its appearance. The body was considered to be a temple. Therefore, your body (or your temple) was to be kept clean and in its natural state at all times, even to the extent that ladies were not allowed to shave their underarms or legs, much less anything else! Nothing was to be put into the body that was deemed unclean or unsafe. You were not allowed to let your body be sick, or this meant you didn't have enough faith and needed to pray and worship harder. Even if one was sick, you were still expected to attend all church services and, of course, go up to the altar to have the laying on of hands and prayer. If you weren't healed once prayer was given, then somehow, you were being disobedient in the eyes of the Lord. You needed to fast and pray or perhaps have your demons cast out, or you needed to figure out where your faith had gone!

My sister and I were quite young when we became members of this cult, so we did not receive all our childhood vaccinations, as this was considered a sinful thing to do to your body. I contracted strep throat. Back in those days, when you got a sore throat, a common home remedy was to take a Q-tip and swab the throat with Merthiolate. Nasty stuff! I can still recall the taste. Usually, it would do the trick, and all would heal. This time, however, it didn't work, and I got sicker and sicker. I remember my dad kneeling over my bed and crying and praying for God to heal me. I ran a really high fever for days and just lay in the bed as I was too weak to get up, much less try to eat. My throat and mouth were on fire, and I was miserable! I eventually got better over a period of about three weeks. Amazingly, I never have had strep throat again. I believe I was just a very lucky little girl, and my guardian angels were looking after me as it wasn't my time to go from this world.

Another time, I woke up and had no feeling in both my lower legs. I couldn't walk. My dad put me in his lap and stuck a needle all the way up both legs, and I just sat there watching in fascination. It just so happens that choir practice was going on at church, and Dad loaded me up in our van and carried me into the church, which interrupted the choir practice. He asked all there to stop and pray for me. Well, they prayed over me so hard, and I could feel the energy of all these people praying for my healing in unison. Suddenly, I felt my legs again. I started squirming, and Dad put me down. Everyone started shouting and joyfully singing. What a moment! It was a miracle! I was healed! I skipped out of that church with my dad and never thought anything else of this incident until later in life when I realized that I had indeed witnessed a miracle. Amazing!

I'm not saying cults are great; but even among all the crazy rules, there is goodness in the universe, even among mixed-up, confused groups of people who just don't know any better!

When I was ten, the preacher convinced the ladies of the church that birth control was frowned upon by God—it was a sin. I recall my mom being very angry about her pregnancy. I vaguely remember overhearing her telling someone that she guessed God wanted her to have another baby, but she wasn't happy about it. I look back on this now and see how crazy it was to trust a preacher with his words of wisdom, telling all the females in the congregation that they would only get pregnant if it was God's will. Come on, people, we all know that the way our bodies are created, if you have sex, you're going to get pregnant! It shocks me in this day and time to think there are preachers out there who preach against birth control as a sin. Do these preachers live in the real world? I had a little sister by the time I was eleven. She was born at home with my dad and aunt delivering her. Thankfully, she was healthy, and there were no birthing problems. It was against our religion to go to doctors. She was weighed in on a scale at our local grocery store, and it was a happy day.

The definition of a cult, according to *Merriam-Webster Dictionary,* is "a small religious group that is not part of a larger and more accepted religion and that has beliefs regarded by many people as extreme or dangerous; a situation in which people admire and care about something or someone very much or too much."

What if the people within this small group begin to create rules based on how they themselves interpret the scriptures? What then? Well, then life within the cult situation becomes even more difficult.

As I recall, during home Bible studies, as the people of the congregation studied the Bible within themselves and these small circles, they began to put their own interpretations on the scriptures. Once an opinion was formed that all agreed upon, it was then presented to the preacher, who certainly did not discourage their thought processes and actually praised them for being even more zealous to worship such a mighty God.

There would be, at times, people who didn't agree with the new rules of worship. I recall my dad voicing his concerns at times; and each time, he would be brought up to the altar and accused of having a demon that needed to be cast out. The deacons would then gather around him and lay hands on him until they were satisfied that all traces of the demon were gone. I realize now this was a fear tactic to keep my dad and all the other members who might question some of the outrageous rules in line. I have often wondered to what end this preacher was striving for. What was the purpose of browbeating people with fear and demons and hellfire? Apparently, this preacher had his own agenda, but to achieve his goals, he needed a flock of followers to do his bidding. His bills, along with all his other expenses, were being paid by the congregation. New cars, a house, etc.—he was living a good life. He managed to get all his "people" to pay their tithes for his own gain. That is for sure!

A few months after my new little sister was born, my dad began having problems with his eyesight. He thought it was because of his advancing age and from working hard. This nagging sight problem slowly worsened to the point that I would be kept out of school to ride with him in his plumbing truck so he could drive to his jobs. The blind spots were affecting how he was able to drive, and he was beginning to have headaches.

One Saturday morning, we were in our van, and Dad went to pull into a gas station. He didn't slow down enough or turn as sharp as he should have, and we ran into another truck. I hit the windshield with my head! No one wore seatbelts in those days. Had my dad not slung his arm across toward me, I would have gone through the window completely. As it was, the windshield broke and cracked all the way across to the driver's side. I wasn't bleeding, and no police or ambulances were called. They just swapped information, and both parties went their merry way.

Dad and I got home. Of course, my parents were concerned but chose not to seek any medical care. There was too much fear about doctors and doing something not pleasing to God, so I was told to go and rest in my room. I believe that accident woke my dad up to the fact that something was wrong with his sight, and he knew he had to do something about it. The next thing I knew, my mom and dad went to the eye doctor to have his eyes checked. Little did I know that my whole world was about to change and crumble into tiny pieces.

CHAPTER 2

THE BIG CHANGE

Dad was diagnosed with a brain tumor. It was so big and invasive that the eye doctor could see it growing just by looking in his eyes with a simple instrument. My mom and the rest of the family were in shock. My sister and I knew something bad was happening, but we were not privy to all the conversations the adults around us were engaged in. I remember during morning prayer (yes, always an hour before school), I prayed for healing for my dad. I was scared. I asked God to heal my dad by giving the tumor to me. I just wanted my dad to be OK.

My heart just ached with fear, but I had another whole thought process going on that no one had any idea about. It was a horrible battle within me that I was so ashamed to even think about saying anything out loud. I knew that the reason my dad was so sick was because I was not being obedient to my elders. I felt it was entirely my fault that my dad had gotten sick! At the same time I was praying for God to give me the tumor and heal my dad, I was also scared that God would do what I was asking and actually give the tumor to me! The guilt was almost more than I could bear!

You see, unbeknownst to anyone, I was being sexually abused by the preacher. One of the threats he used to keep me in line was that my family members would get sick and die if I didn't do as I was told or instructed to do. He told me God would punish me, my family members, and anybody else I loved and cared about if I didn't comply. I can recall many times I just didn't want to do what this man was insisting I do, but I was too scared of God and the punishment to not do what I was told. I had been exposed to way too many demon services and seen too many things in my short life to not believe these things could really happen. Now, all of a sudden, my dad was sick with a really bad brain tumor!

I was convinced it was my entire fault. God was angry with me for not being a good girl. If I had just kept my feelings hidden better and sucked it up! If I had not resisted the touching, the squeezing—if I had not complained! God was so angry with me! All these thoughts were going around and around in my head, and I felt like everything was spinning out of control!

Such horrible guilt for a child at the tender age of eleven. My innocence was stolen by someone claiming to be a man of God who used fear of God and consequences to keep me in line! My dad being diagnosed with a brain tumor sealed my fate for an ongoing battle to overcome a horrific fear of God. I didn't feel comfortable praying anymore. I was too scared to pray. It was like I always felt God looking over my shoulder, shaking his finger at me, and whispering in my ear that I better be good or He would swoop down and get me. "I got your dad. Now, who's next?"

Shortly after Dad's eye appointment, he went to Oklahoma City for brain surgery. My sister and I weren't told much. Everything seemed very hush-hush about his illness. I remember not going to church as much or seeing many people we used to see almost daily. It was like, all of a sudden, the church people had disappeared. My little sister was only about two months old, and my mom was staying in the city with Dad.

My aunt stepped in to help take care of us girls while my mom traveled back and forth to the city. My grandfather snuck me into my dad's hospital room a few days after his surgery. His head was all bandaged up, and there were tubes everywhere, but I wanted to see my dad! I walked up to the side of the bed. I looked into my dad's eyes, and without a word, I knew he didn't recognize me. I could see the confusion in his eyes and the pain. He didn't know who I was! My heart fell to my feet as I stood there looking at this man lying in the hospital bed. He tried to speak but was unable to form any words. The sounds he made were guttural and unfamiliar to me. He seemed to become agitated, and I suddenly felt a hand on my arm as my grandfather pulled me away from the bedside.

I felt the shame of all my bad deeds settle even more heavily on my shoulders as I looked at this man, whom I loved so much, suffering because of my "bad" actions and disobedience to the preacher and God.

My grandfather must have realized the situation was getting out of hand, and he got me out of there pretty quickly, but the damage had already been done in those few moments I stood at that bedside. I knew without a shadow of a doubt that God was something to fear and obey, or bad things would happen. My precious dad, as I knew him, was gone from me forever.

Life became blurry for a while as we all struggled to cope with such a major illness. I went to stay with Mom and Dad in the city while my dad took cobalt treatments for six months. My sisters stayed home with other family members. Thankfully, the brain tumor was benign (noncancerous), but radiation was needed to ensure there was no further growth and that Dad would be able to live a healthy long life. I wish I could give you a happily-ever-after story for my dad, but after twenty-five years of medical issues, he finally succumbed and passed on due to complications from his brain tumor. He was fifty-nine years old.

The remaining years after his surgery were, at times, a struggle for him. He remained a humble man of God and helped his church family to the best of his ability. He was my dad, and I cherish all the happy memories I have of the love and affection he gave me as a child.

Once brain surgery and radiation were done, life changed dramatically. We didn't go to church anymore. This felt strange to me to have so much free time on my hands, but I also felt lonely.

My mom had her hands full dealing with raising three girls, taking care of Dad, dissolving his plumbing business, and getting us signed up on welfare. My mother had not worked outside the home for years, and all of a sudden, it was up to her to provide for us all. Dad was totally disabled and could not work. He had frequent seizures, speech issues, mobility issues, and thought-process issues, on top of taking different therapies to try to gain back so many of the things he lost from having surgery. I'm sure this had to be a very stressful time for my mother.

We never saw any of the church members again. They totally dropped association with us because we had gone against the rules and gone to the doctor for my dad. Family members helped us put food on the table, along with many of my dad's old plumbing customers. Such generosity from total strangers! Even though a brain tumor had robbed our family of our sole provider, people stepped up and helped us when we needed it the most, and the majority of these people didn't go to church! Where had all the good Christian people gone? How could they just turn their backs on our family?

We finally managed to receive welfare and food stamps, and eventually, Dad began receiving Social Security disability benefits. For a while, it was a rocky road for my mom as she struggled to keep our family together in one piece. I have no memories of even one church person, much less the preacher, helping our family during our time of need.

In my mind, there were no more church services or church people because we had broken the rule of "no doctors." It was like being shunned for doing something we weren't supposed to do according to God's Word. Our faith should have been strong enough to heal my dad without going to the doctor. Even though times *were* tough and my routine had changed, I had a sense of relief that I didn't have to be around that preacher anymore because I never liked him at all! I had carried that feeling I had about the preacher for several years, and my feelings had not changed. I had just "squashed" them so I could survive in his presence. I didn't realize that I would carry these feelings I had stuffed into adulthood and beyond as I made decisions about my life.

The Tennessee Way

Once things had begun to settle down a bit from Dad's illness and my Mom was slowly getting a handle on being head of the household, the decision was made for our family to move to Tennessee. This was the summer I had turned twelve, and I was *not* happy about being uprooted. I had one friend. One friend! She was the only constant in a topsy-turvy world, and I adored my friend Suzanne. She accepted me and my weird ways of living without question, and I didn't want to leave her! She never made fun of me or picked on me. We rode our bikes all over Elk City together and just had good, clean fun together. When my long skirts would get caught in my bicycle chain, she would help me get untangled, and off we would go again.

My mom would allow me to go and spend the night at Suzanne's house occasionally, and we would play with no fear of getting into trouble. We would always spend Friday nights together, and when we got up on Saturday mornings, the TV would be turned on with cartoons. I had been taught TV was really bad, so I tried hard to not look at the screen. My curiosity got the best of me one time, and I actually watched for a few moments from the doorway but was too scared to go into the room and sit down. I was scared God would get mad at me, and I would go to hell! I didn't want to tempt fate by looking at the screen too long, but my goodness, how I wanted to see Daffy Duck and Bugs Bunny!

Spending time at Suzanne's house gave me small glimpses of a different way of life. Suzanne and her mom wore pants and seemed fine to me. I enjoyed spending time with them because it gave me a break from the stress of my religious life. When the day came that we girls were sat down and told we were moving to Tennessee, I just cried and cried! I didn't want to leave my one friend. How would I cope? Who would I talk to? What would I do?

Life was about to get scary again.

We moved to Tennessee in the summer of 1977. It was a hot long drive, and as we got closer to the mountains, I got motion-sick from all the curves and up-and-down motion. I was used to the flat lands of Oklahoma with miles and miles of flat bear grasses. As we drove through Arkansas, there were wildflowers everywhere. It was beautiful! There was every color one could imagine, and the trees were getting thicker. As we drove across the Tennessee line, the trees caught my attention. They were so lush and green! They were everywhere! The landscape started getting curvy, and the hills began to get bigger and bigger. We finally arrived at a rented trailer in Greeneville, and there were trees everywhere. It all seemed so very different to me, and the humidity was so thick you could feel it on your skin. I was used to a very dry heat in Oklahoma.

Now I felt really angry! I was forced to leave behind everything I knew in Oklahoma and come to a place that made me sick in the car from all the hills and curves; the crappy humidity made it even worse! I was at a very low point in my life. I just didn't see how being in this new place would be any different than where I had come from.

Time seemed to move very slowly that summer. I sought refuge in the acres of woods around the trailer park. I would wander in the woods for hours until dusk. I knew I had to be in before dark. It was cool under the canopy of trees, and it was peaceful and quiet. Mom and Dad were busy scouting for a house to buy and trying to figure out what town to live in and settle into. Greeneville was just a temporary stop to our final residence. Finding a good church to attend was a top priority, along with a decent school district for us children.

My aunt and uncle had discovered a small church in Johnson City. It was similar to what we had come from but better. The adults decided to check it out, and we all went to our first service. Once the adults agreed it was a good church, it was decided that we settle in Johnson City to be close to our church family. We found a rambling old house suitable to our needs and moved in with no major problems. Life was looking up! A nice home, a good church, and a good school district! Finally, maybe things would begin to settle down, and life would become normal again.

As it neared time for school to begin, Mom started the process of getting my sister and me registered. Well, guess what? It was against the law in Tennessee for children to attend school without all their vaccinations! Oh, brother! I thought, *Oh well, we won't have to go to school! Yeah!* School had always been painful for me, although I made good grades. I just struggled with looking different and believing in no holidays and such, but lo and behold, my mom took both of us girls down to the health department. The next thing I knew, I was getting all these shots and vaccines in one day! I was confused and angry. I lost track of how many shots I got that day. Why was it now OK to get all these medicines when it wasn't before? I couldn't wrap my brain around it, and quite frankly, there were so many changes happening in my family I was afraid to question why. That just wasn't something children did back in those times. We were to be seen but not heard. Obey our elders, and don't question anything! So I kept my mouth shut and

CHRISTINE PETERS

took my shots. Painfully! This was yet one more reason to hate living in Tennessee.

The school year began, and I was terrified! This school was much bigger than what I was used to and had twice as many kids attending as my old school. I stood out because of my unusual clothes: long skirts, long sleeves, hair in a bun, etc. No one looked at me or spoke to me. It's almost as if I was invisible. I felt shy, uncertain, angry, and vulnerable. It was not an easy time. In elementary school, recess was three times a day, and this was considered enough exercise; but in this new school, PE class was required, and the students had to wear a one-piece uniform that was shorts. I had never had to show that much of my body in public before, and I felt panicky that first day when I found myself in PE class. I knew that once again, I was going to have to stand up and show my religion to the teacher and in front of the whole class.

To be honest, I was more worried about having to wear something that showed so much of my body because I had gotten used to covering my whole body. I felt ashamed just thinking about other people seeing my bare arms and legs. I even hated it when my mom came into the bathroom to scrub my ears in the bathtub. The shame I was beginning to feel just thinking about strange boys and girls seeing me in shorts in a PE class was unbearable to me. The next day, my mom sent a note to school with me to give to the teacher. Thankfully, I was dismissed from PE and allowed to work in the library during PE class.

The library opened up a whole new world to me. I had never been allowed to read anything fiction, so when I discovered Nancy Drew and autobiographies and so many other wonderful reading materials, I was just engrossed and kept my nose in a book all the time! I had found a way to escape safely without punishment and have some fun. I still love to read even now and encourage everyone to try it. You just might like it!

Once I discovered reading, my grades improved, and I even began to enjoy some aspects of my schooling, like English and social studies.

There were many changes my family went through during the summer of '77. Moving to Tennessee, finding a new home, and attending a new church—it was a lot of change in a very short time. Things were beginning to settle into a semblance of a routine once school started, and my anger was slowly subsiding as I adjusted to being in Tennessee.

My sister and I came in from school one afternoon and knew immediately something was different. Mom and Dad had bought a TV! I was shocked! We had been taught that TV was wrong and sinful, and now we had one in our front room! I felt confused yet happy at the same time. I never thought to ask why. Who was I to argue? That evening, we all sat around the new TV, had popcorn, and watched *The Wizard of Oz*! All the colors and the music! I was totally engrossed with the whole experience. What a wonderful way to introduce your children to something new. Even now, as I write this, I still remember the excitement. I can feel the pleasant memories flood through my being. It was wonderful and amazing! At that moment, all was well with the world, and any fears of consequences from God were gone. I blocked out my fears of whether God was going to punish me and just sat back and enjoyed the show.

It was clear to me that I needed to sit up and pay close attention to the preaching at church. I felt I must have missed something along the way. I tried to remember a sermon when our new pastor preached about TV being OK but could not. Once again, it never occurred to me that I could approach the pastor and ask him about having a TV. After my last experience with a preacher, I certainly didn't want to draw any attention to myself by approaching our new pastor with any questions. I knew I was to be seen but not heard, and I was taught to never question anyone with authority over me. This new church we attended had a lot more members than the church we had come from, which made it easier to not be noticed by anyone. This was fine by me!

Christmas was fast approaching, and one weekend, Mom and Dad sat us down and got into a discussion about having a Christmas tree in the house. Mom wanted one, but Dad felt it was worshipping a graven image. I sat there silently, waiting to see what the decision would be. This was an important family decision that had to be made with all in agreement. It was a big deal. I had looked at Christmas trees in stores and windows, but we never had one in our house that I could remember. My mom wanted to do a tree for us girls, but Dad pulled out the Bible and began reading different scriptures out loud in protest of any tree in the house. There was some arguing to be sure. I continued to sit there silently, and finally, it was put to a vote. Needless to say, my dad lost, and we got to have our first Christmas tree when I was thirteen.

I'm thinking by this time that our new church isn't as bad as our last church and that maybe I can be good enough after all to keep God happy and go to heaven.

CHAPTER 3

GROWN-UP CHOICES IN A CHILD'S WORLD

The winter of 1978 brought with it flannel slips and lots of snow. Much to our delight, the first heavy snow resulted in the schools closing. My sister and I weren't used to this happening. In Oklahoma, you went to school in all types of weather, so a snow day was a real treat. We could sit at home and watch TV all day or read or play and just relax.

In eighth grade, I was allowed to join the choir. Oh my gosh, they sang music that wasn't gospel! This was a first for me. All I had ever been exposed to was gospel music or music in a movie. I had not been allowed to play any kind of music except gospel on the piano, so being in the choir opened a whole new world for me. I loved the beat and the four-part harmony! It was just so beautiful! I would take the sheet music home with me and teach myself how to play it partly by the music and partly by ear. It gave me great joy to make my piano sing with that music. It was nice to expand my world with other kinds of music. I never thought to question my mother about why I was suddenly allowed to play something other than gospel. I just felt grateful to have the opportunity.

That same year, I was allowed to compete at school. I enrolled in the national spelling bee and won three times in a row! I received a trophy and two savings bonds. It was the first time I experienced the thrill of winning and feeling proud of what I had accomplished.

It was during the summer of '78 that tensions seemed to escalate between my mom and dad. Dad was still struggling with being disabled and not working, and my mom was still finding her feet trying to raise us girls and hold everything together. The new church we attended was much more liberal than the old church, and my dad was having a hard time with the lack of rules. There were many arguments about God and religion and what was right and wrong. At times, it felt like the floor in our house was made of eggshells. I spent lots of time in my room sleeping or reading, as that was my only escape from the tension. The differences between the two churches seemed to create conflict in our family. My dad seemed stuck with his mindset from the church in Oklahoma, and my mom was trying to move us forward and adopt the beliefs of our new church.

In my mind, it seemed as if God wanted one thing, Mom wanted another thing, and Dad wanted another thing! It was very confusing to me! Out of all the things that everyone seemed to want, there was one thing they all agreed upon. That was that we all need to be rebaptized. I had already been baptized once in Oklahoma, and all of a sudden, it was like that baptism wasn't good enough. We needed to do it all over again but differently somehow. As we all sat around talking about it, I just nodded and acted like I fully understood why this needed to be done when it really made no sense to me. Why was one way better than another way? But as usual, I kept my mouth shut.

We made a date for the whole family to get rebaptized, and I figured, well, why not? What would another dunking underwater hurt? The new pastor rebaptized all of us. By this time, I was so confused about why it should matter so much, but I knew better than to ask any questions. It was just easier to go along with whatever the family decided and stay silent.

I never even noticed that I had gotten or fallen into the habit of not thinking for myself or asking questions like why. It was such a simple question, but because I had been punished for asking why at such a young age, I had learned to keep my mouth shut and my feelings to myself lest God punish me for speaking out of turn.

CHRISTINE PETERS

Once a person gets baptized, I was taught to "seek the Holy Ghost." You cannot go to heaven unless you get baptized and get the Holy Ghost. This is taught in lots of different churches and religions. However, there are lots of different versions of what the Holy Ghost is to different people. I was taught that one must stay humble and cry a lot, begging and pleading with God to grant one this gift while on your knees at the altar. This praying, crying, begging, and pleading on one's knees also usually included people around you, praying for you and touching you and crying and asking God to grant you the Holy Ghost so you will be saved and go to heaven.

The main sign that one received the Holy Ghost was that they would suddenly speak in another tongue or language. If you didn't speak in some sort of gibberish, you had not received the gift of the Holy Ghost. When one finally spoke in tongues, everyone else would start jumping around and shouting up to the heavens, thanking God for the gift given to this humble person still kneeling at the altar. It was exhausting just watching this experience, much less participating!

My experience of getting the Holy Ghost happened when I was nine. I went to the altar and began the ritual of crying and praying for forgiveness and then started begging for "the gift." I cried because I was scared that I would go to hell if I didn't do what everybody else was doing, and I was tired of being scared and thinking I was going to go to hell for not having the Holy Ghost. I knew getting this gift was expected of me, and I didn't want to disappoint my parents.

The child that I was, I wanted to do what had to be done to keep God, my family, the preacher, and anybody else who knew me happy. I thought if I didn't try to do this, I would go to hell when I died. It was all I had ever been taught. My tears were real that night. I cried because I was scared. I was scared that God would be mad at me if I didn't try to receive his Holy Spirit and scared that I would grow up to be a bad person with demons inside of me if I didn't just try to receive God's Holy Spirit. Up to this point in my life, I had been taught that God was outside of me and up in the sky, looking down on me. No one had ever told me that God was already in me, with me, part of me—that my soul was a piece of God that I already had from the moment I was born! My soul, your soul, and everybody's souls are a part of God! That light we call our soul is "God within us"!

Somehow, I had taken on the belief that God was this judgmental big being who would only be good to me as long as I lived by all the rules that the preacher, society, and people of authority told me I had to follow!

As I cried and prayed at the altar that night, I had made up my mind that I wasn't leaving that altar until I got to speak gibberish too! Several hours went by, and I began to feel very tired. Even though I was concentrating on continuing my crying, the people around me called the preacher over to anoint me with olive oil and to ask God to grant me my request. I was trying to make my lips stammer like I had seen other people do. I was aware enough to sense the preacher coming toward me to place his hand on my forehead. He began praying over me and jerking my head with his hand, almost like he was trying to force this gift to come into me! Each time he jerked his hand, I could feel my neck and shoulders snap with the force of his touch. It startled me so bad that he was being so forceful that I just opened my mouth and started muttering gibberish so he would leave me alone and stop jerking my head!

I continued letting gibberish come out of my mouth, fully aware of what I was doing. I had seen other people do this many times. When things began to quiet down a bit from all the dancing and hollering, I slowly quieted down myself and eventually opened my eyes. I was done. I was exhausted but happy that everybody around me was happy and that I had gotten the gift they always talked and preached about.

Did I feel any different? No.

I finally had a piece of God in me, but now I had a new fear. What was I going to have to do to keep it there? I discovered pretty quickly that I still had to live by the same rules. I began to wonder, What about all the other people around me who didn't go to church? What about them? Were they all going to hell? What about all the other people who went to other kinds of churches? Were they going to hell? It was all just very confusing to me!

By the time I entered ninth grade, my mom and dad had divorced. The stress from my dad's illness, along with all the church rules, had taken its toll on our family; and life, in general, seemed stressful and unkind. Sometimes just the circumstances of life can chip away at a peaceful, calm existence, and suddenly, everything seems to fall apart. I have to admit that when Mom sat us girls down to tell us they were divorcing, I felt a great relief. There had been so much tension in our home for so long that I had gotten into the habit of spending all my time in my room. I slept a lot as I was deeply depressed but didn't realize it at the time.

Never once did it occur to me to question God about why my family would fall apart. I was living with the guilt of my dad's illness as best I could, and at times, I would be able to not think about it and squash it out of my mind. I secretly thought that it was my entire fault because I was just a bad girl. Deep inside, I constantly battled guilt and shame. I just accepted that all these bad things were happening because it's all I deserved in life, and I did the only thing I knew how to do: I squashed all my feelings down because they were too hard to deal with. Anyway, who was I going to tell? I had reached the point that I felt like God didn't listen to me anyway because I was such a bad person! You reap what you sow—or so I had been taught from the Bible.

During the time my parents were going through a divorce, my mom quit going to church. She never gave any explanation, and I never asked. I just noticed it but said nothing. I began riding the church bus to attend services. Mother never stopped me, but she never encouraged me either. Again, I never questioned her decision. I also never directed any anger toward God. I was too scared. The fear was real.

My mom suddenly had to learn how to drive and had to get a job once the divorce was final. She and my older sister began wearing pants and tops with shorter sleeves. None of these changes were ever openly discussed. I continued attending church and riding the bus, living by all the rules I had been taught and thought I had to do to be a good person. A good Christian.

My mom was under a lot of stress. She took a job from three to eleven, and we became latchkey kids. It was hard on her trying to keep the roof over our heads and raise three kids. My older sister got a job to help supplement food and bills while I babysat for my younger sister.

As a new school year approached, I got involved in a program where you could go to school half a day and work half a day. My grades were good, and I stayed in this program until I graduated from high school. I worked two jobs during the last two years of school and managed to buy myself a car and pay for my own insurance.

I had never really made any close friends at school. I had become a loner and didn't mind my own company. I stayed busy, and eventually, life got in the way of going to church. By the time I graduated, I had pretty much stopped going to church. Quite frankly, I didn't miss it. I was busy trying to make money and better myself and just pay the bills. I put the whole God thing to the back of my mind and never looked back. It was time to just make a life for myself and decide what I wanted to do with my life.

I quit going to church, began wearing pants and shorts like my mom and sister, and never looked back. I do recall the first few times I wore pants, I felt really odd and worried about God getting mad at me, but I had finally reached a point in my life that I had begun to not care. I was what Christians called backslidden, and I was more than likely on my way to hell! I felt at that time that I just didn't care whether I went to hell, but I did care about whether the bills were paid and there was food on the table. I realized that I couldn't be perfect because it was too hard, and for once, I just wanted to have some fun in my life!

Shortly after high school, I married my high school sweetheart. I was trying to do what I thought was right: get married, work, and build a life with someone. We were both so young, and neither one of us was ready for real life. We were children trying to be adults. Reality hit hard when I discovered I was pregnant. I had so many unfamiliar emotions going through my head, and I felt scared and vulnerable. Worst of all, my body was changing, and I had no control over these changes.

I was angry that I had something growing in my body. I felt violated! This was not a good feeling for me. I never said anything about these feelings out loud, but when my mother and husband sat me down to talk about what my options were, I jumped right on the idea of an abortion.

My mother was supportive, and so was my husband. He wasn't ready for the responsibility. I look back now and wonder if my mother somehow sensed my inner turmoil and how upset I was about my body. I didn't know at the time, but I had repressed all the memories of sexual abuse. I didn't understand why I was feeling the way I was feeling. I just knew I had to get rid of this "thing" inside of me as quickly as possible. It would be several years before I discovered the damage that had been done to me emotionally by being sexually abused by the preacher of that church so long ago.

As it was, my marriage lasted all of six months. My husband was a good man, but he just didn't understand me and didn't want to understand me, so he began stepping out of our marriage vows. I can't say that I blame him fully. I was very immature and childish, and in all honesty, I didn't know myself well enough to have a good relationship with any man, much less a marriage. When he came to me and sat me down to tell me he wanted a divorce as he had found someone else, I was upset but also secretly relieved. On what would have been our first anniversary, I was in divorce court in front of the judge. I look back on this episode in my life and realize he had done me a favor by divorcing me. With the mindset I had about myself and God, we would have lived a miserable life. I can't imagine how awful a child's life would have been had I carried through with my pregnancy.

CHOICES AND CONSEQUENCES

I wish I could tell you that I made all good choices as life went on, but that would be far from the truth. I attended college for a few semesters but quickly discovered it just wasn't my thing, although I did make a lifelong friend while there. I cherish our friendship even to this day as I write this book. She has encouraged me and, at times, scolded me for not getting it done sooner!

I married again after being divorced for four years. I didn't want to get married. I wanted to run away, but my mother grabbed my waistband and told me it was too late to back out with so many people there to witness the event. I was actually half out a window when she grabbed me. I felt panicked. The marriage was doomed from the start. The man I married had a horrible drinking problem, and I came very close to being arrested for him writing bad checks on our joint checking account. Since I was the one who had opened the account, I was considered the main account holder. I had added his name after we married.

As the relationship began to fall apart, we went to counseling as a couple. I was determined to make it work. After three sessions, however, the counselor suggested my husband do individual counseling, which he refused. He felt our problems were all my fault. I certainly wasn't blameless by any means, but his constant lying and alcohol abuse didn't help matters. We hadn't discussed children prior to our wedding, and I was religious about birth control as I didn't want a repeat of what I had gone through in earlier years. I had never thought about all the volatile feelings I had felt during my first marriage and pregnancy anymore. I had just ignored the feelings and squashed them away. It was all I knew to do with them. I also knew by this time that I had no desire to have children. I had convinced myself I would be a terrible mother and mistreat any child I had. I never questioned why I felt this way. I just knew I did. Quite frankly, I was terrified I would hurt my own child. I had no idea that my early upbringing had instilled this thought process.

I had been married for about six months or so when I began having some health issues with my bladder. I went to the doctor and was sent to a urologist. I was sent to Florida to enter a medication trial for people with these same issues. The medications taken for my condition were all narcotics, and I had reached a point where I was taking them like candy. The side effects were terrible: dry eyes and mouth, blurry vision, lack of sweat, and sensitivity to sunlight. I had to be really careful during the summer to stay out of the sun. On the days the meds didn't seem to work well, I would still go to work; but it was painful to walk, stand, or move. The only relief I got, if any, was to sit in a hot tub of water and soak.

I had yet another doctor's appointment, but for once, it was for my yearly OB/GYN checkup. I always dreaded going to the OB because I still struggled with having to take off any of my clothes in front of strange people, even if it was a doctor's office, and I certainly hated the exam part! Imagine my surprise when the doctor came into the room and informed me I was pregnant! My first thought was *Oh no! This can't be!* I had always been so careful about birth control as I knew I had no desire to have a child!

My doctor recognized that I was at high risk for issues with this pregnancy, so I was sent to a high-risk OB to see what could be done about the other health issues I was having. I began having all those horrible feelings again of being violated on top of the pain of the bladder issue. The feeling of violation was so strong it was overwhelming, and I felt ashamed and guilty and so many other things it is hard to put into words.

I was scheduled to have an ultrasound within a few days, so I went home to give my husband the news. I was not a happy camper but was hoping that perhaps the doctor could give me something to help with the pain I was having so I could continue to work and get some relief. I was bringing in a steady paycheck that paid all our bills and rent. My husband only worked sporadically, and his check was always garnished for child support.

When my husband came in that evening, I quietly told him about being pregnant and that I was being sent to a high-risk OB as there seemed to be a few problems with the pregnancy that had to be checked out, according to my regular OB. He was overjoyed at the prospect of a child and immediately told me to quit my job and stay in bed to be able to carry to full term. I couldn't believe what I was hearing. Did he not realize that without my steady paycheck, we wouldn't be able to pay our bills and the rent and buy food? Who was this man, and what planet was he living on? I immediately began arguing about what a bad idea that was, and he began treating me like I was the worst person in the world to worry about such "stupid" details. I was so angry at this point I was speechless! I just had to walk away at that point. I realized quickly that if I didn't figure this one out, I was going to be homeless with a baby and no way to provide basic needs for this poor child that, in all honesty, I was afraid to have.

I went to the appointment with the high-risk OB within two days. After another ultrasound, he came in and told me there were malformations. I should do a D&C immediately. I could miscarry the child, but if I waited, it could endanger my life. A D&C was safer. I thought about it for a few moments and then asked them to schedule the D&C. I had no problem making this decision as I already knew I would be a terrible mother. My body was also in pain from the bladder issue. I had taken so many narcotics for the bladder problem. This was probably why the pregnancy wasn't normal.

As the adult I am now, I realize I was so horribly abused as a child that my thinking was skewed. As the person I was in my early twenties, I knew I would not be a good mother. I was terrified I would somehow abuse any child I might have, and I didn't want to put a child in that position. God forbid that I be selfish and have a child whom I might abuse physically or emotionally. I just couldn't do that to another person. It was almost as if I was punishing myself with a childless life because I thought I was a terrible person and could never be good enough to deserve a child who would love me.

Needless to say, my husband called me every profanity he could think of when I told him what had to be done. He informed me that I was a murderer and he would never forgive me. Shortly after my D&C, I left him and went my own way. I just couldn't deal with his judgment and drinking. I suddenly saw a glimpse of myself and my future, and I knew if I stayed with him, I would never amount to anything or be a productive person. It was time for me to leave.

A few days after our divorce was final, my ex-husband called me so he could tell me what a rotten wife and person I was and how nice for me that I could just turn off my emotions like a light switch. What he never saw were the bitter tears I cried at my friend's house the day I left him. I sobbed so hard I choked on my own saliva and just felt so lost and all alone. Once again, I had married someone who couldn't comprehend the person I was. I couldn't fully understand or comprehend the person I was, either.

There was a comment he made that stuck in my mind for a long time: "It must be nice to turn your emotion off like a light switch." What did he mean by that? Had I turned into such a cold person that I didn't have any feelings anymore? For the first time, I tried to take a good long hard look at myself and examine my thoughts about the comment he had made, but it just didn't make sense to me. My feelings were hurt by what he had said, so surely, that meant I had emotions, right?

I got involved in another relationship pretty quickly after my divorce. We moved in together. He wanted to get married, but I was hesitant. I had finally found a career I enjoyed and was concentrating on improving my skills and learning all I could about my trade. I was feeling fulfilled with my career and was putting all my heart and soul into what I did for a living to the extent that I always put my work first. It was a safe haven, where I could express myself through my creativity, and it made people happy.

I had become a floral designer. The shop I worked in was busy and sent out good-quality work. The owner was a successful businessman, and I admired how he ran his business. I watched him like a hawk and learned everything I could. In a sense, my boss had become like a surrogate dad to me. I would have done anything to please him. He was very critical of my work for several years, but when a new person was hired, he would pull me aside and offer me another ten cents on the hour to train them. I settled into a routine and just worked while avoiding my family obligations to my mom and sisters.

During this time, I got sick and had to have surgery unexpectedly. At the time, all I was told was that I had a tumor in my arm, and it was growing so quickly that it probably had some "bad cells." Bad cells? Was this cancer? I asked. The neurologist looked me in the eye and simply said yes. My heart sank. All I could think about was whether I would come out of surgery with my arm intact. The surgical team was talking over my head about taking nerves from my leg to place in my arm to perhaps get some mobility. I had lost the feeling in my arm within days of discovering the lump. I felt scared. Things were out of control all of a sudden. I was scheduled for surgery within a week and arrived at the hospital early on a Thursday morning to check into my room. Thoughts were spinning around in my head. What would I do if I lost my arm? How would I play the piano? How would I be able to design flowers? How would I pay my bills?

Thankfully, the tumor turned out to be a ball of pus, which required surgery and lots of antibiotics with a drainage tube. I was in hospital for a week and very weak but regained my strength quickly. It was just a freak infection that, thankfully, had not gotten into my blood. The doctor who came to see me after surgery told me how very lucky I was to be alive. If the sac of infection had burst, I would not have survived.

This experience changed my perspective on how I was living my life. I began to see that work wasn't everything and that I needed a better balance between work and family. I needed to make a decision about what my priorities in life were.

I made the decision to marry again. He had security and a job and could provide me with insurance in case I got sick again. I was so tired of trying to survive on my own! I thought if I could just have some security! We got married in the front room of his house one evening after work, and then, everything changed. I found myself being treated like I was a piece of furniture. Something to be paraded around to friends and out in town. I thought I would be safe because this man didn't go to church. He just worked and played. He had lots of man toys—a boat, Sea-Doos, a limo, an RV—and endless rounds of partying with his rowdy friends. All the while, I continued to work, clean the house after all the endless parties, and cook dinner every night. I did the laundry and spent the weekends on the lake. All these things seemed endless! I enjoyed it for a while until I didn't.

The problem with this lifestyle is that it's great at the time, but it wears thin after a while. The late nights were getting in the way of my work life, and I would drag myself to work tired from a weekend of staying out too late and drinking. I discovered that drinking was a great way to avoid all the feelings running around in my head that I didn't know how to handle, and I was on the fast track of becoming a full-blown alcoholic. My husband was happy to supply me with all the moonshine I wanted because he could give me a drink or two and then engage me in sex for his benefit. It reached a point that he would greetme at the door each evening, asking me if we were going to have sexthat night. I felt the only reason he married me was so he could make me dress up, go out, party, and then have sex every night. It was awful!

My husband worked in auto body and fiberglass repair and had a bad habit of not bathing. I wasn't thrilled to have sex with him because he never bathed, and this was unpleasant to me. I always struggled with sex, anyway, as I felt dirty every time I shared my body with my husband. All I wanted at this stage in my life was to have a home with quiet, happy times and not too many people around. My husband asking for sex every night at the door when I came in was making me feel used, threatened, and vulnerable. He was triggering my abuse issues that I wasn't even aware I had up to this point in my life. I had buried all those memories.

Now, I realize that sex can be a wonderful and intimate act between two people whose chemistry is good and both agreeing to engage in the act and share with each other. However, that was not always my experience. I struggled with feelings of being dirty after intercourse. I always thought everybody had these feelings. In the era I grew up in and the culture then, sex was not openly discussed so I never questioned other women about their experiences. I would go take a bath immediately after having sex. I didn't question why I had these feelings. I thought it was a normal part of life. My husband never questioned why I acted the way I did. He had no way of knowing that the sexual act was a very real struggle for me. It was all I could do to perform in the bedroom. I was getting to the point of actually hating having to have sex. I just did not see the attraction of the sexual act. I reached a point where I just couldn't handle having sex every night. I felt too dirty and unclean. My husband began to verbally abuse me because I wouldn't have sex every night. He began drinking heavily and partying with people much younger than him. He would stay out late in the night, and I would be asleep when he would finally decide to come home each night. I recognized that my marriage was falling apart slowly but surely, and I didn't know what to do to keep it together.

The summer I was thirty-two, I received an invitation from my one girlfriend in Oklahoma to come out and make flowers and play music for her parents' fiftieth wedding anniversary. I was pleased with the invitation and told her, of course, I would be there. I figured it would be a good break from the stress of my marriage, and I was looking forward to seeing my old hometown and visiting my friend.

This would be the first time I had been back to Oklahoma since I had moved as a young child. I decided to drive out to Oklahoma. During the drive, it occurred to me that I was on the same interstate we had traveled so many years ago when my family moved to Tennessee, feeling like an angry kid and knowing that I was moving away from all that I knew. As the miles rolled by, I let my mind wander to the early years of my life.

The oddest thing happened as I was on that drive. As I got closer to Elk City, I began to feel a tight knot in my stomach. It was very uncomfortable, and I tried to shake it off. Eventually, it went away, but the negative feelings inside myself were hard to ignore. When I pulled into my friend's driveway, I was calm and ready to help her throw this party for her parents.

It was wonderful to see my friend again but awkward at the same time. We had stayed in touch through the years but had not seen each other in person for many years. We talked late into the night, just catching up on each other's lives. She filled me in on the details of the anniversary party and then told me that some of my family members wanted to see me while I was in Oklahoma.

I was a bit surprised about family members wanting to visit with me. These were people from my dad's side of the family, and I didn't really know them very well.

I got up to a bright, sunny morning, and plans were made on how to spend the day. One of my uncles picked me up and began driving around town, showing me all the old haunts of where we had lived; my grandparents' house; and, finally, the church we had attended. The morning of the party dawned bright and clear. It was a beautiful Sunday morning. I had agreed to go to church with Suzanne and her family since the anniversary party was to be held in the fellowship hall immediately following services.

We pulled into the parking lot, and as we found a place to park, I began noticing all the people dressed for church walking toward the building. Everyone was wearing dresses and seemed so intent on getting inside the building. All of a sudden, everything I was looking at went into slow motion. I realized I suddenly felt sick to my stomach and broke out in a cold sweat as I sat there, trying to make myself move to get out of the car. I could hear a loud buzzing in my ears, and a hot flush of heat spread all over my body. My hand froze on the door handle, and I began feeling a panic like I had never known before. I was taking in deep breaths of air, trying to regain my composure, when my friend Suzanne opened the door for me. She knew immediately something was wrong. I looked up at her and just shook my head no. I couldn't move, much less go inside that building. I was just too scared! The term *frozen with fear* took on a new meaning for me that fateful day. At that moment, I came to the realization of a literal fear of God.

I managed to eventually go inside the fellowship hall for their party, but there was no way I would go into the sanctuary. As I recall, I sat in the car for the services and met up afterward to celebrate at the anniversary party.

Somehow, I made it through the rest of my trip. I could hardly wait to get out of Elk City and back to Tennessee. The entire visit to Oklahoma had left me with a disconnected feeling that I didn't recognize at the time, but I could feel that something was off within myself and my body. I couldn't get out of that town fast enough. I drove back to Tennessee like the hounds of hell were on my back bumper. I remember thinking how comical it was that, as a child moving to Tennessee, I was full of anger and hate. Now, I was more than happy that I lived in Tennessee as an adult. I reached home sixteen hours later and carried my luggage in with a sigh of relief. Safe. I was home safe. Everything was going to be OK now.

I settled back into my old routine with work. Every now and then, I would feel that disconnected, uneasy feeling, but I kept pushing it aside and ignoring what was happening. My dreams at night were disturbed and fragmented. I was having nightmares, but awake, I had no memories of what I was dreaming. I just knew they were nightmares, and they left me feeling awkward and vulnerable, although I didn't understand the nature of these feelings. I just recognized that something was off.

My husband was still fussing at me about sex. He was threatening to look elsewhere to satisfy his desire. I was scared he was going to tell me to leave, and I had nowhere to go. I didn't make enough money to put a roof over my head, and my mother had already told me that I would be on my own if this marriage didn't work out. I would be out on the street.

During all this turmoil in my personal life, a new employee had been hired in the shop where I worked. He wasn't from Tennessee originally, and I was drawn to him like a moth to a flame. His personality was so open and friendly, and he seemed quite comfortable talking about any subject. It was interesting talking to him as he had wonderful stories of things he had done in life with theater and music. I was fascinated by all these unique stories he would tell us about as we worked making flowers. I mean, this man could talk about any and everything with ease, and there was never any judgment or condemnation. I had never been around anyone before who was so open-minded. Therefore, I enjoyed working with him, and we became fast friends. I called him my work husband, and I will forever be in debt to this man for being there for me when I needed it the most. I believe he was sent from above to help me at a time when I was unable and unprepared to help myself.

My workday began just like any other workday. It was a busy day, and everyone was rushing around, working on orders and making sure everything was being done in a timely manner. There was never a dull moment in the busy flower shop, and our crew of seven was talking and laughing as we furiously made up flower arrangements for delivery. Everyone always staggered our lunchtimes so as not to interrupt daily timed deliveries.

On this day, Dale and I were on lunch break at the same time. I was telling him about my trip to Oklahoma and the struggle with my home life. I got tearful as we were talking. At this point in my life, it was quite unusual for me to show my emotions to other people. It was something I was taught as a child: Do not show emotion in public. One must take care of things without showing any emotion. I was uncomfortable letting anyone see me get emotional, but on this particular day, I couldn't seem to hold my emotion inside; and here I was, crying in front of my coworker!

We clocked back in from lunch and got to work. I was struggling to contain my emotions. Dale was working on the table beside me, and he would glance over at me occasionally. I reached the point that the tears were silently sliding down my cheeks. I continued trying to work, but my tears were blinding me. I felt ashamed, and I didn't even know why I was crying. I wasn't able to stop the tears, and even though I hadn't made a sound, my friend Dale knew there was more going on in my mind than what I had voiced during our lunch break.

He quietly came and stood beside me. He took me by the hand, led me to the privacy of the back office, and sat me down. I was sobbing openly by then. All I could do was look at my friend and cry! He got me some Kleenex, and while I was blowing my nose, he got the phonebook out and began looking for numbers of counselors in our area. He recognized I needed some help. I was sobbing so hard by this time that he had to speak to them and get me an appointment. Thankfully, by the time an appointment was made, I knew I had somewhere to go for some help; I began to feel calmer and was able to finish my workday. I had no clue what a personal counselor meant, but I was about to find out rather quickly that this was the beginning of a long and difficult journey to uncover my deepest and darkest secrets about my life and, most importantly, God.

When I got home from work, my husband greeted me with his usual "Are we going to have some sex tonight?" I felt like screaming! What was wrong with me that I couldn't bring myself to comply? I was very thankful that he never insisted I comply. I'm not sure how I would have reacted if he had insisted. Instead, he would get angry with me and shout insults toward me to try to shame me into giving in to his demands. I had grown used to the abusive words and the shouting. I felt I deserved it for saying no; I was harder on myself with my own inner dialogue than he would ever be with the shouting and insults. Once again, I realized I had chosen to be in a relationship full of abusiveness. I vowed to myself to work as hard as I could to make this marriage the last, and I was at my wit's end, trying to juggle the pressure I was under. I was glad I had an appointment with a counselor. I hoped she could "fix" me so I could be happy and feel some peace within.

Life goes on—until it crashes.

BEGINNING THE JOURNEY

I arrived at the counselor's office with a few minutes to spare, feeling nervous and sweaty. I wasn't sure what to expect, but I knew I needed some help to sort things out in my mind. I was convinced at this point that there was something very wrong with me. It felt as if my whole life was falling apart suddenly.

My first two visits were full of tears, sobbing, and an abundance of Kleenex as the counselor asked simple questions about my life and childhood. One thing was abundantly clear: my marriage was falling apart, and I felt it was entirely my fault. The counselor suggested that perhaps my husband would like to come in for a visit along with me for a time or two. I thought this was a wonderful idea and was looking forward to going home and asking him to work with me to make our marriage better.

The reaction I got when I spoke with my husband was a slap in my face and a curt "Christine, if you continue to see a counselor, you need to pack your bags and get out immediately." He was extremely angry and told me if I would just spread my legs more often, he would treat me better and not make me leave. I was devastated. I grabbed my suitcase with a few clothes and went to stay in my sister's basement until I could figure out what to do.

When I got to work the next morning, I was called into the back office, where I was fired for having an affair with my boss. I was shocked and never saw it coming. What a joke! I was struggling to have sex with my husband and hold my marriage together while being fired from a job I loved for having an affair with my boss. I look back on this and have to laugh. Sex was the last thing I cared about. Now, my husband ditched me, my boss ditched me, and I was homeless, all in the space of twenty-four hours. My whole world had unraveled in the blink of an eye. Rock bottom had arrived. There was nowhere else to go but up from here.

Journey's First Step

I began going to counseling once a week. Even though I didn't have a lot of answers, it did seem to help me stay calm. Something inside me realized this had to be done. I began to understand that knowledge was power. I began to see that I needed to understand why I thought and reacted to certain things the way I did. Many times, while exploring different aspects of life events, I was intrigued to discover many gaps in my memories from childhood. My counselor, Ladonna, would ask specific questions about different things, and I would try so hard but just could not bring up any memories to be able to answer her questions.

It was during this time that my mother and I were living together. My mother had always kept a journal. I began asking her questions about my childhood, and she offered to let me take some of her journaling so my counselor could piece together more of my childhood.

Ladonna began to read; and within a few short moments, she laid the papers aside, looked at me, and calmly stated, "So you were raised in a cult for a partial time during your childhood?" I looked at her and immediately started getting defensive and telling her how normal my childhood had been. How happy I was as a child—blah-blah-blah. She stopped me and then gave me the definition of a cult: "a relatively small group of people having religious beliefs or practices regarded as strange or sinister."

Oh boy, my brain started thinking about the long dresses, no jewelry, no TV or radio, no makeup, no cutting of your hair for women, and all the other rules I had lived by as a child all the way up to my late teenage years. I left that session with a flood of memories bubbling up and out, and for the first time, I felt the stirrings of anger. Anger at God! But then, just as quickly, I pushed the anger toward God down, knowing the consequences would be harsh if I allowed myself to feel angry at God.

You see, I had lived for thirty-two years believing God loved me but would punish me if I did the slightest thing wrong!

Ladonna worked with me for three years once a week to lovingly teach me that I could make choices without risking punishment from God. The day I realized that I really could make my own choices without having to seek approval from others was a big lightbulb moment. As my counseling continued, through hypnosis and eye movement desensitization and reprocessing (EMDR) therapies, I began to have flashbacks of some very unpleasant things that had happened to me.

All these unpleasant things seemed that God was punishing me, and no matter what Ladonna said, she was unable to change my mind. Eventually, I overcame enough of my fears that I had my ears pierced and got a haircut. It took several years of baby steps for me to be able to see the whole picture, and I had made up my mind I wasn't going to quit counseling until I felt fixed.

Throughout the beginning of this counseling process, in the background was my friend Dale. I would share things with him about my sessions if I was struggling to understand what Ladonna was trying to teach me. He never judged, but he was always able to give me a different perspective about some of the things I was learning. In essence, he was helping me to think for myself!

Dale was attending night school for a degree from college, and one of his classes was psychology. He was given an assignment to write a paper on something out of the ordinary and how it affected one's life. He chose religion as his topic. He approached me to ask if I would mind him interviewing me for this paper. His subject was religion from a cult point of view.

I agreed to an interview. We sat down one day after work, and the questions began. I don't recall the questions, but I do remember he got an A on his report, although one lady in his class became angry and walked out during his recitation. He thought it was interesting as the woman was dressed in a similar fashion to what I had as a child.

CHANGING THOUGHT PROCESSES

As my counseling continued, I was beginning to see how being exposed to religious or cult things had been ingrained into my being from the very start of my memories. Any choices or decisions I tried to make seemed to reflect what I knew about life, which was very little, honestly, except a God who would punish me if I didn't do good. This was always my first thought about anything I thought about doing in my life. How would God react to the decisions I made, and what would He do to me if I didn't make the "right" decision?

When this came out in my counseling, it was very clear that I had a lot of work ahead of me to deprogram everything I thought I knew about God.

It also became very clear that my mind looked at all preachers as if they were God, which meant anything they preached about or said was gospel to me and had to be obeyed. I actually believed that anything they preached or said was actually God telling me to my face that these things have to be followed or I would go to hell.

During a discussion one day about how I felt about wearing pants, I immediately started quoting scripture to my counselor. I had this one memorized: "A woman shalt not wear that which pertaineth to a man" (Deuteronomy 22:5). I argued that, yes, I was wearing pants and would go to hell for it, but that was God's word. It was the Bible! No one questions the Bible! Why would I question the Bible? That would be wrong. I could get punished really badly for questioning the Bible. The Bible is God's holy word!

Ladonna simply looked at me and said, "Christine, who wrote the Bible?" I stopped my ranting for a moment, and silence filled the room. Who did write the Bible? God? The apostles? Matthew, Mark, Luke, etc. Men. They were men. Human beings. Just like me. People who are not perfect. My mind started racing with thoughts I had never allowed myself to have before.

Was it OK to question myself about the Bible and step out of the box I was in about God? This was when I slowly began to realize the following:

- God creates us all with free will.
- God creates us all to be able to think for ourselves.
- God creates us all to feel for ourselves.
- No one is perfect.
- We each are able to have our own walk with our Creator without another human being telling us how we must live.

I felt a small weight lift from my shoulders once I realized that going to church wasn't the only path to having God in my life. I do have to say here that society teaches us to think that if we don't go to church, we are not good Christians and are not going to a good place when we die. During this session, it finally clicked in my mind that I had indeed been brainwashed into believing all the rules and consequences of God and that I had been living my life in the most unusual way. Every decision I tried to make about living was based on a fear of what would happen to me if I didn't choose correctly. In other words, what would God do to me if the right choice wasn't made? It still had not occurred to me that my choices were my own. I still carried the belief within that God had control of every choice I made when, in fact, we are all created with free will and can make any choice we want. It has nothing to do with God at all!

You would think my thought process would change immediately once the above came into my mind, but sadly, this did not happen.

Instead, these new thoughts only created more questions in my mind, which I would realize later were like a never-ending loop of negativity.

Now that I understood how skewed my thinking was, I was more determined than ever to continue my counseling to discover more about myself and how my thought processes were working in my head. I told myself I was finally "healed," and now my life was going to be lived happily ever after. Boy was I wrong. I still had a lot more work to do. And so the real journey began.

CHRISTINE PETERS

CHAPTER 4
THE REAL JOURNEY BEGINS

CONTROL ISSUES

I didn't realize how much control played such a role in my life. Without any thought, if I was feeling bad about something going on in my life and had not been able to change the outcome, I would dive into a project and not stop until I was done. Instead of pausing for a moment to allow myself to feel the feeling of not having control, I kept myself so busy I chose to just ignore the feeling and not deal with it at all. A good example would be cleaning and scrubbing the entire house to the point of exhaustion and redusting a few hours later because I saw more dust lying on the tables. This was how I coped with all those feelings of not having any control. The satisfaction of accomplishing a task made me feel better. The harder the task, the better I felt. All the cleaning had to be done perfectly. This was the only way I could feel like I had some control over my life.

Thankfully, whatever situation in my life would eventually resolve itself on its own, or I would finally have to make a choice. Any situation will always work out the way it is meant to be. That is just life; however, at the time, I always tried to control how every situation ended. This wasn't a realistic way to live, but I didn't understand that during this time. I found myself having anxiety and nervousness with every little decision or situation in my life because I never felt like I had any control.

I eventually learned that sometimes, by not making a choice, one is making a choice. When we choose to not make a choice, for me, it was because I was afraid of any choice I would make. I had no confidence in myself to choose wisely. Therefore, I often found myself in situations that were not good for me and where I wanted to be in life. Making a fear-based choice was all I knew because of what I learned in my religious upbringing. This is not to say that every choice I made resolved the situation the way I wanted it resolved; rather, when I tried to control the situation, many times, it would turn out negatively, like my marriage.

I would pray—asking God to help me, my marriage, etc.—while thinking that I was a bad person because I didn't go to church anymore. My thinking was that God wouldn't hear or listen to my prayers because I wasn't in church anymore. I felt I wasn't worthy to be heard!

Once again, I was making myself a victim of my own thoughts because of what I was exposed to as a child about God. I really believed at the time that I would not be heard and that I, as a person, did not deserve to be heard. Carrying such a belief in my mind was very damaging to my self-esteem and confidence. It created depression and anxiety; therefore, I was always looking for confirmation from people around me that the choices I made were good instead of taking a moment to focus on what I was feeling about any decision I might make about my life.

INTUITION

I recall a few sermons about the washing of the feet. The church we attended would have foot-washing services, and we would have to pick someone out of the congregation whom we had "bad" feelings or thoughts about and ask them to allow us to wash their feet as a gesture of forgiveness. I was so young I would have to think really hard to come up with a negative thought about someone in the crowd so I could "wash" their feet. Then, as I watched the grown-ups around me, I saw that they would pray, sob, and ask for forgiveness from God. I never really understood the entire purpose of this ritual. It didn't make much sense to me to purposely think something negative just so I could wash someone's feet and ask for forgiveness. I just remember how hard I had to think to come up with something—anything—so I could participate. I thought if I didn't participate, I was a bad person. I was too young at the time to understand that my inner guidance, or intuition, was showing me this was a silly tradition; but because I wanted to please God and my pastor and parents, I ignored my gut and instead thought up a silly thing about a person I hardly knew to participate in a ritual that actually had no meaning except to flood myself with a negative emotion for which I could then "forgive" myself for having the negative emotion. Had I listened to myself, I would have sat out of this ritual; however, in the situation I was in, it was looked down on when you didn't participate.

What did this teach me? It taught me to ignore my feelings and do what outside influencers told me to do. It didn't matter what I was feeling or thinking. What mattered was that I participated along with the rest of the crowd. This is so wrong on many levels. When we choose to ignore our own feelings, we are choosing not to honor ourselves. We must honor ourselves first and foremost before we honor others. If we all did this, the world would be a different place.

Intuition is an important part of who we are as human beings. We are all born with intuition. It is "built in" to each and every one of us. I had not thought about this word or its meaning until I got deeper into my journey with counseling.

Intuition is one of the most important aspects of each individual. You'll hear someone say "I felt it in my gut" or "I just had a hunch." The reason intuition is so important is that it is an inner compass to help steer us along our path in life. When we ignore our intuition, we can find ourselves in some tricky situations. Our intuition is the inner guidance that helps us define what is right and what is wrong. We can "feel" this sensation when we stop to pay attention to our bodies.

Children are more tuned in to their intuition than we are as adults. By the time we reach adulthood, we have been exposed to extreme amounts of outside influences in our lives (religion, radio and TV, and social media). We become accustomed to listening to all these outside influences instead of taking a moment to focus on our inner feelings and listening to our own thoughts. When you combine all these with the added drama of religion telling you we are born into sin and will go to hell, it creates fear within you. On top of that, you hear messages about just how awful hell is with all the fire and brimstone. We begin to make decisions based on the fear of what God would want us to do. I have to make the right choice so God doesn't need to send me to hell!

It is quite a vicious cycle, and we don't even realize we are doing this torture to ourselves because we are so brainwashed to listen to all the outside influences of those around us whom we have been taught to have authority over us and what we think and feel. The reality is that *you* are the only one who can know exactly what you are feeling and thinking. *You* have the power of choice and free will to do whatever will be good for *you*.

Let's take a moment to stop and think here. Ask yourself this simple question: what purpose is there to send a person to hell for all eternity to burn in fire and brimstone? Do you really think God or our higher power who loves us totally and unconditionally would do this to one of his children? If you have children, and you have the power to determine what their lives would be like after they passed over, would you send your children to a place like hell? Of course not! And God wouldn't either!

Now, as you ask yourself these questions and ponder the answers, put your focus on what is going on with your body. Do you feel sadness? Are you crying in sadness thinking of your child in hell? Do you have some goosebumps because your mind is trying to grasp such a simple scenario that perhaps we have all been victimized into believing that people go to a place called hell?

I have come to the conclusion that hell and the threat of going to hell is just a scare tactic to keep people in fear from living their lives fully. We are being bullied into believing nonsense when, in fact, there is no such thing! Stop and think about this. If there is no hell, how would that change how I live my life? Allow yourself to feel the wonder of letting go of the fear of hell! Isn't it magnificent?

We have all been taught to look up into the heavens and seek God. When we pray, we automatically look up and raise our arms into the heavens. We have been shown to look up and reach out to God. Instead, we should be looking within. We are all born into this world with our higher source within us already. We are created this way automatically.

Our intuition and our feelings are one and the same. We are born innocent and free to experience anything we choose to experience and be able to learn and grow. What we are exposed to begins to shape or mold us into the adults we become. Unfortunately, when we are exposed to negative aspects like religion, societal images, politics, and money, we can get off track of the wonderful human beings we start out being. Then it becomes our challenge to remember who we are before all the bullshit of life! This is our journey and our purpose of being.

Remember, intuition is never wrong. Your feelings are never wrong. Listen to your feelings, and they will never steer you wrong. When you attend church, if the speaker says something you're not sure about, pay attention to what you are feeling. If any authoritative figure in your life encourages you to do what they tell you and not follow your feelings, stop and question within your mind. Don't just follow their advice. Focus on what *you* are feeling and then make your decision accordingly.

We are created with feelings for a reason. Don't ignore them. Instead, honor them. You will find that life will become easier when you honor your feelings. Society and religion have been telling us for too long to ignore our feelings when we should be doing just the opposite.

GOIN' WITH MY GUT

I was still continuing my personal counseling and had changed careers as I had become disillusioned with my former choice. I made this career change because my gut had given me so many feel-good feelings that I knew I had to do it. If I didn't, I would not feel joy again. I chose to listen to myself and continued concentrating on working on myself to feel a better balance with my mental health. Things were humming along, and I felt happy and fulfilled with my choice to try something totally different.

It was during this time that I began dating a man I met through a coworker. He was quite different from the other men I had dated, and I was drawn to him like a moth to a flame. Rather quickly, he began talking about marriage. I thought about it and felt the strangest feeling that I had to marry this man because he was going to teach me a lesson that I needed. I also knew that the marriage wouldn't last long but that

I had to marry him to learn my lesson. The feeling was so strong that I couldn't ignore it. I still didn't trust myself or my feelings, but I just knew I had to do this. So we went to the courthouse and got married after only a few months of dating.

We started out just like any other married couple. We found a place to live and settled into our lives. Prior to marriage, he had never shown any interest in going to church and never talked about his faith. In fact, I don't recall us ever having a conversation about God or our feelings about religion or God.

I came in from work one evening, and he was cooking dinner. Before I knew it, we were having a discussion about religion, and he told me he had decided to be a youth minister. He informed me I would be the "dutiful" wife and play the piano and help him minister to the young people in a church he had decided we would start attending. When I began telling him how I felt, he began quoting Bible scriptures at me and telling me that by marrying him, I had agreed to obey him in all things. He became angry when I voiced my concerns and pinned me down on our couch. He got up close to my face, and as he gritted his teeth in anger, he informed me I would obey what he said because it's what was in the Bible!

I felt fear at first because of the anger in his voice and body language, but then, I felt a calmness come over me. I firmly asked him to get out of my face. When he stood up, I got up and turned around to face him. The emotion I felt was a very strong confidence within myself as I told him, "No man—*no man*—is going to tell me how to serve God, and *no man* is going to force me into doing something I feel I am not qualified to do. I will not be responsible for influencing the life of a child by teaching them anything about religion!"

Of course, he had no idea of my background because I had never shared my childhood with him. I just recall that when I spoke my truth, he sat down on the couch and just looked at me with so much anger on his face. I didn't back down. Eventually, he got so angry that he walked outside. When he came back in, it was like nothing happened, and the conversation was over. I knew that was my lesson, and I had learned it well. *No man*, no matter who it is, will ever again teach or tell me how to best serve God, my higher power.

CHRISTINE PETERS

I immediately recognized that this argument was a wonderful gift given to me and a very powerful moment in my life. I had broken through the chain of my personal belief system, which is to do everything a "man" (i.e., a person of authority or a preacher) told me I had to do or believe. Talk about a feeling of freedom! I had a sense of freedom I had never felt before. I also realized immediately this was my lesson. No man or anyone can really know how to serve God any better than anyone else because we are all just guessing at it and doing the best we can. None of us will know until we pass from this body back to the spiritual realm we were created from, how best to celebrate our connection with God. What a glorious time that will be when we leave this body behind to go be with our higher power!

Shortly after this argument, the marriage ended. We divorced, and I never looked back.

CHAPTER 5
KNOW THYSELF

I found myself a little studio apartment in a quiet section of town where I could heal from all the bad marriages and continue to work on myself and my mental health. Obviously, I felt I was still making bad choices, as here I was with yet another failed relationship.

I had started journaling when I began counseling, and I had gotten into a daily habit of writing down my thoughts and dreams each evening before I went to sleep. Many a night, I would sit and cry. I felt so lonely, but I had made up my mind I was done with men. I just couldn't handle it. All men wanted was to hurt me, control me, belittle me, and abuse me—and I was just done! I look back on this time and realize I was finally breaking a cycle of choosing abusive men. I was finally putting myself first by remaining single. I was finally beginning to heal some of the abusiveness I had experienced from men. It was an abuse I had gotten myself into because I had such low self-esteem. I still continued to believe what I had learned at such a young age that I was a bad person and that God thought I was a bad person. Unbeknownst to me, I was still living my life thinking and feeling that my higher power had no desire to help me, much less hear me, if I chose to pray because in the back of my mind was a recording telling me I was not worthy to be heard. Clearly, I had more work to do on myself.

I lived in this tiny studio apartment for several years; and I shed many tears of loneliness, fear, and sadness. I was experiencing heavy depression but continued to work each day. I was just "enduring" life rather than living to the fullest and feeling joy. I found a safe space and was content to stay there while I continued counseling.

During this time, I had to transition to a new counselor. This was hard for me as I had learned to trust her, and I was scared of going to someone new. However, as always, there was a higher power than me at work, and it was time for me to move on in my journey of self.

The first session with my new counselor was totally different in how she approached all the issues I obviously needed to work through. She was definitely not like my first counselor at all! She had a tough-love approach and wouldn't allow me to wallow in pity for myself. Laughingly, I would have to say we had a love-hate relationship! I was quite stubborn in many of my beliefs, and there were a few times I would slam out of her office, vowing to never go back! I always went back after I had time to process what we had discussed, and I always had more questions. She was trying to teach me to think for myself while also teaching me to look within. I was starting to get the knack of thinking for myself, but looking within was a much different matter. I was too afraid to look within, and I didn't trust what was within myself because I had been taught first by religious beliefs and then by society to always look outside of myself for answers to everything. I did not trust any feelings I had and basically had learned as a child and the school of hard knocks to totally ignore my feelings.

I was never taught to put myself first. I was always taught to put God first. You know, the Big Man upstairs, the higher power way up in heaven, looking down on all of us and having an opinion on every little thing we say and do in life. I was taught it was a sin to put myself first. I was taught my feelings didn't matter, but what God felt about me was what I should worry about. When you have to worry about what God is thinking or feeling about you, it puts a lot of pressure on you. How are any of us supposed to live perfectly? We are human, and I haven't met anyone yet who is totally perfect, have you?

This new counselor had her job cut out for her. Years later after meeting me, she confessed that I was a tough nut to crack!

The list of all the things I wasn't taught could go on and on. Aside from overcoming spiritual abuse, we all need to learn to become our true selves as much as possible before we die from this physical body and move on to the spiritual world.

FORGIVE ME!

Religion teaches us to pray and ask for forgiveness from God, but during this process of prayer, do we remember to forgive ourselves? I never did in my younger years. Let me give an example.

When my dad was diagnosed with a brain tumor, I can vividly remember praying and asking God to "please take this tumor away from my dad and give it to me." During several sermons, I can recall the preacher saying that if we have enough faith, we will be healed. He also preached that if we prayed hard enough, we could ask God to give us the sickness to spare the ill person. Then, if we had enough faith, we could pray the sickness away. I also recall the thoughts in the back of my mind as I said this prayer asking for my dad's tumor. I was scared I would receive the tumor and then not have enough faith to get rid of it, and I would die. Then, I felt guilty for having the thought that I didn't want a tumor in my brain. Then I felt the guilt for feeling the guilt. It was awful! All this guilt just because I wanted my dad to be all right and not be sick! The level of shame I felt was off the scale. I had all these negative feelings because I believed what this preacher was shouting from the pulpit. I was a small child and believed everything I heard. I carried these feelings of guilt and shame for years!

The worst of these feelings came from the fear that my dad's illness was my fault because I resisted complying with the preacher who was molesting me. He would tell me God was going to punish me or my family members if I didn't let him touch me and defile me. I thought I was being punished by God because I put up a fight with the preacher molesting me. I also thought God was punishing my dad because I wasn't being good and obedient to the preacher. I had no way of knowing how twisted these thoughts and feelings were and how damaging all the preaching was to my psyche. All I knew was that the God I was taught about was loving but would punish too. God could also be harsh and judgmental but love me all at the same time.

Because of the experiences around me with my dad, I felt as if I was being punished by God because I was disobedient. Once again, the fear of God was ground into my mind and soul. How could I ever forgive myself for being bad and having bad thoughts when bad things were happening to my dad? Forgiving myself was not even a glimmer in any of my thought processes! My thinking at the time was that if God would even think about forgiving me, I would have to buckle down and do everything I was told with no resistance—period. The punishment to my dad was so scary—so severe—that I could not imagine how much worse things could be if I didn't do better.

If God couldn't forgive me, then how on earth could I possibly even begin to forgive myself? With all these thoughts going through my mind, along with feeling so much fear of the consequences from God, I just shut down and felt nothing but numbness for years. Unfortunately, this experience only solidified how scary God was and how awful the punishment could be if one didn't do what they were taught and told to do.

It took many sessions of counseling to overcome the shame and guilt I carried about my dad. I did heal from these things; however, my fear of God and self-forgiveness would elude me for a few more years.

The act of forgiving oneself is one of the hardest things to overcome. We are our own worst critics and are quite good at browbeating ourselves with guilt, shame, and all those other negative thought processes we are taught as children by religion and society. Even though these feelings are negative, it pays to take a look at them when we feel them bubble up to our awareness.

One of the first steps in forgiving yourself is to ask yourself why you are having this feeling of _____. Too many times, this is where we stop because the thoughts or images that come to mind are too painful or the feelings overwhelm us. Let's face it, sometimes, feelings can be very unpleasant; and quite frankly, it can be scary to allow ourselves to feel these strong emotions. Or even worse, we have been taught to squash any feelings that would cause us to look at our behavior because we might feel shame, remorse, or guilt for even having a feeling like that. Can you imagine feeling shame and guilt for feeling shame or guilt? What a contradiction, right? How different our lives would be if we just allowed ourselves and learned from an early age how to honor our feelings.

As I look back on my early childhood, it is clear to see how I entered into survival mode to get through my childhood. Once you allow yourself to pay attention to your feelings and understand why you are having them, you may find that the feelings are valid. This will make it easier to forgive yourself if that is what is needed for you to feel better. We all must learn to honor our feelings and accept our feelings to heal and move forward. Forgiveness is a form of acceptance. If you struggle to forgive yourself, then just accept yourself, and forgiveness will come on its own.

Praying to ask for forgiveness for myself was the last thing on my mind with all the other turmoil going on around me! Many years later, I was finally able to forgive myself; and then several years later, I realized there was nothing to forgive. I was a child enduring horrific abuse mentally and physically, and none of it was my fault! Once the realization that it wasn't my fault came into my awareness, life began to change for me. I began forgiving myself easily and being kinder to myself. What a freedom this provides!

Now, I know it's easy to write these words about forgiveness; however, I have found that telling myself "I forgive you" and *feeling* the forgiveness are two different things! I believe that one must acknowledge feelings in the mind first and then come to an acceptance of these same feelings. Then, with little to no effort, you begin to feel the forgiveness in your heart.

As I continued my personal growth, I began to see and feel this pattern, and I began moving toward my growth more rapidly. When I acknowledged my mistake and accepted it, I immediately felt several different emotions all at one time. I learned to feel the emotions and honor them. Then, inside my mind, I gave myself permission to express the emotion in a safe environment (my home or the counselor's office).

The act of forgiving oneself will be with each and every one of us for our entire lives, as none of us are perfect. We mess up all the time! We are supposed to. This is how we learn about ourselves and life.

Just remember to be kind to yourself when you goof up. Stop all the harsh criticisms! When you accept yourself, the forgiveness of yourself becomes much easier.

Even as I write this book, I recognize that I have more work to do on myself; and every day, I realize I continue to have a fear of God. This seems almost silly in a way, but for someone who was raised to fear God and listened to many sermons of hellfire and brimstone, along with the graphic details of all the different monsters from Revelation, this literal fear of God can be a big hurdle to overcome.

LOVE THYSELF

The church I grew up in preached about vanity and what a sin vanity can be. My understanding of vanity ties in with pridefulness. It was implied that if you loved yourself too much, that was being vain; and therefore, one could go to hell for being this way. These teachings translated into the women of the church were not allowed to wear bright colors, makeup, clothing that would flatter their appearance, and fancy hairdos. They were not allowed to shave hair from their legs, and the list goes on and on.

It would have been considered vain and prideful to wear a dress with, let's say, sequins or too many ruffles or any kind of hair bow that was decorative or shiny, and never in a million years could you color your hair! How crazy is that?

I always thought I loved myself, but as I got deeper into my journey of self-discovery, I realized I had been depriving myself of love by following all these crazy rules! I had already made up my mind I was going to go to hell, so in my thirties, I finally started wearing clothing with a bit more color. I found I felt quite conscious at first and that I stuck out like a sore thumb in a crowd, but I wore what I wanted to wear anyway. It never occurred to me to question myself about why I felt so conscious about wearing bright colors. I guess it was my way of rebelling!

Take a moment to think about how you treat yourself and how you make choices about what you wear. Are you wearing items just to wear them? Or do the clothes you pick to wear give you joy? Such a simple thing but so very important! Do you actually despise wearing a dress?

If so, then why do you continue to wear one? I understand now that God doesn't care about what you wear. What matters the most is that we acknowledge that there is a higher power and allow ourselves to connect to God.

Let's do a quick test to see if you love yourself. Go to the closest mirror in your home and stand in front of it while looking yourself straight in the eye. Now, as you look into your eyes, say "I love you" and mean it. Now, set the book down for a minute and do this exercise. It wasn't as easy as you thought it would be, was it? Did you find yourself feeling silly or laughing and unable to meet your own gaze in that mirror? Did you have a feeling of "This is silly! Of course, I love myself"? Or did you feel like crying because you couldn't bring yourself to feel serious for a moment and feel the love? Did you feel yourself struggling as you tried to meet your own gaze? What feelings did you feel when you looked in the mirror? Now is the time to be completely honest with yourself. It's just you and the mirror. How do you *honestly* feel when you look in your eyes in that mirror?

When my counselor gave me this exercise to do at home, I thought she was crazy! Of course, I love myself! I'm a good person! The first time I did this exercise, I found out quickly how hard it was. I had a lot of feelings, all right, and none of them was love! I realized I couldn't look myself in the eye and feel any love at all. As a matter of fact, I actually couldn't even look myself in the eye! Talk about a rude awakening!

I was totally baffled by why this was a so difficult exercise. It seemed such a simple thing, but for the life of me, I couldn't meet my own gaze. Actually, I felt no love at all. Love was nowhere to be found that day! I tried off and on all week to do this exercise, but I just wasn't feeling it. I did, however, reach a point where I cried at myself in front of that stupid, hateful mirror!

Needless to say, I had to get several more counseling sessions under my belt before I came to the realization that accepting oneself is a form of self-love. I had to overcome the thought that I was being vain and prideful by loving myself. You see, all the teachings about vainness and pridefulness had twisted in my mind; and I was afraid that by being vain (taking care of myself) and being prideful (taking care of my appearance), I was committing a sin. I would be punished by God and go to hell if I loved myself. If one takes a moment to think about these types of teachings to children, it can create confusion and plant seeds to not love themselves.

In my experience, religious teachings and societal impressions taught me at a very young age to not love myself because to do so would make me "vain," "prideful," or "not humble." This also teaches a child not to value themselves, by teaching a child that it is a sin to do anything to make yourself pretty like wearing makeup or fingernail polish. When a child is told that God "looks down" or God "dislikes" a person for this, that, or the other, it teaches the child that "God doesn't like this, so if I do these things, I won't go to heaven." In other words, one will go to hell for doing the things God doesn't like. The child is being taught that God will punish them if they don't follow the rules. In this instance, the rules include "Don't make yourself look pretty, or you might be considered vain or prideful or, even worse, not humble." Remember that phrase in the Bible about being humble in the eyes of the Lord? In my experience with religion, if they are preaching about heaven, then hell is being preached too. I don't know of any religion that preaches about hell being a great place, do you?

With so many rules to worry about and follow, how in the world can anybody manage to be holy in the eyes of the Lord? I reached a point when talking about this with my counselor that I felt exhausted relaying all the rules I was supposed to live by. I made a conscious decision that it was just impossible to remember, much less live, by all the rules, and I would just have to go to hell! I just couldn't do it anymore. I was exhausted! Nobody I knew could live up to all these expectations! Not even my family members.

Making that decision was a turning point for me. I decided to live by the Ten Commandments and forget the rest, as it was just too complicated. When I made that decision, I slowly began to love myself finally. I began to slowly live life the best I could. I still had plenty of conflicts going on in my mind. I still felt that God didn't love me or hear me, yet when life got hard or problems came along, I would still try to pray and ask for guidance. In the back of my mind the whole while, though, I always had the thought that if God couldn't love me as I was, then how in the world could I love myself?

I lived several more years with this thought and just tried to get through each day. I didn't realize I wasn't living. I was surviving. It's two different things. Living and surviving. We'll save the living and surviving for another chapter for now.

ACCEPT THYSELF

Let's go back to the mirror for a moment. While you are looking in the mirror, notice all the random thoughts that come to mind. "I'm too fat," "My hair is crappy," "I hate my nose," "I wish my lips were fuller," etc.—these thoughts are a vicious cycle of negative "tapes" that we play to ourselves to keep us from loving ourselves. Most of the time, we don't even realize we are doing this. By quietly listening to these thoughts and *believing* these thoughts, we are not loving ourselves. I'll be the first one to stand up and say how hard it is to accept all the imperfections I have in this life. God knows I am *not* perfect! Who is? Nobody! So now, instead of acknowledging all these negative thoughts, how about stopping the first negative thought, turning it around, and allowing yourself to say something positive about your nose or your hair? This is the beginning of acceptance. I know accepting oneself is hard, but it can be done. Once you accept yourself or things about yourself, forgiveness starts to come naturally.

For me, accepting myself is more about appreciating what I have. I then express gratitude for these aspects of myself. For example, I have "mousy" thin brown hair. I am still as good of a person as anyone else, even though my hair is not what I would consider beautiful. Sometimes you just have to acknowledge the good and the bad; and besides, a hundred years from now, nobody is going to care what color or texture my hair was when I'm dead and gone! Hopefully, when I leave this earth, I'll be remembered for my actions and how I treated others. Nobody will stand at the funeral home and say, "Oh, her hair was so mousy!" Of course not! I laugh out loud writing this sentence!

I have discovered that accepting yourself is all about the attitude you have about yourself. If you choose to think of yourself in only negative ways, then it is harder to come to an acceptance of yourself. Acceptance is a choice. Let me repeat that: acceptance is a choice. To reach full acceptance, one must acknowledge the good and the bad parts.

Another thing to accept is your feelings. When you accept your feelings, you, in essence, are honoring yourself, which is a form of self-acknowledgment and self-love. When I finally acknowledged to myself that I had a literal fear of God, it was my first step in healing. As the process of allowing myself to feel these feelings of fear progressed, I discovered that the things I had been taught about God were coloring all the negative things I felt about myself.

I like to think about it in other terms now. My past thought process was "I make so many mistakes that God will be unhappy with me, so therefore I am not a good person, and I am going to hell." My healthy new thought process is "I am a part of God who created me, so therefore, God loves me unconditionally, which means I can love myself unconditionally because I am a part of God, and God doesn't make mistakes!" Remember, God sent his Son to earth, and He knows all the struggles we go through. He doesn't expect us to be perfect. He wasn't perfect while He was on earth, so why should we expect ourselves to be perfect? As far as all the rules our religious leaders keep telling us we have to follow, I now believe all these rules are man-made. After all, the men (apostles) who wrote the Bible are humans, just like me. What if they interpreted a few words wrong? Who is to say they got it perfectly right? The Bible is a book that has been translated so many times now that common sense tells me there are bound to be words that were changed. The reality is that none of us will really understand God until we pass over from this earthly plane into wherever we go after we die.

CHAPTER 6
FINDING MY SOUL

There are many books written about the soul. Of course, the Bible talks about the soul throughout its pages, but do you really "know" your soul? I didn't! When I reached a point in my mental and emotional health that I started thinking about my soul, I began questioning things in my mind. I had been taught many things about my soul as a child and then later as an adult, and I thought I was in pretty good shape when it came to my soul. I knew I had one. Everybody has a soul. At least, that's what we are told and taught by religions, our elders or parents, and society. I thought I knew my soul from all the preaching I had heard and then later all the books I read off and on about souls and the journey of the soul. In reality, I discovered as I allowed my mind to think about my soul that I was as scared of my own soul as I was about God! Why? Because I knew my soul was tied in with God, so to speak, and I was still carrying around that hateful "fear of God" thing I couldn't seem to shake.

So just what is the soul? It seems so distant and, at times, abusive. How does one really meet one's soul? These are questions I began to ask in my mind as I slowly began to open my wounded heart from years of fearing God and everything God represented to me. I knew my soul and God were tied together somehow, yet it still eluded me to fully understand my soul and the role the soul plays in living a life of contentment and peace.

Sometimes, when we put a question in our minds and really want an answer, God will use any number of things to help us learn and grow on our journey. Along with the questions about my soul, I began to question if there really was a God. I mean, everything I was taught in religion as a child was so scary and "hard." It seemed to me that God had so many consequences. Was God really this demanding and scary? Did God really have all these rules? Why do so many bad things happen?

By the time these thoughts began coming to my mind, I had reached a point where I felt the need to be by myself and "hibernate." After my last disastrous marriage, I was fed up with relationships and decided it was easier to be alone.

I found a cute little studio apartment and settled in for a nice long stay. I worked, I went to counseling, and I came home. I didn't have much money for "extras," so I didn't have cable TV. I found myself sitting a lot, journaling my thoughts and feelings. I spent three years in this tiny apartment, with my main focus being my mental and emotional health.

It was during this time I discovered I was having a problem with food. I mentioned this to my therapist, and she suggested going to my internist to speak with him about this issue. I had reached a point where I couldn't swallow any solid food. I was drinking Ensure but was just skinny as a rail. I went and asked the doctor to give me something to help me eat, which led me to then set some appointments with an eating disorder specialist. I found it interesting that as the specialist got to know me and my background better and it became obvious that my eating habits were caused by fasting as a child in the cult and survival, this therapist flat out told me she couldn't talk to me about God or anything with religion or spirituality. When I realized what the problem was, I was able to heal the rest of the way on my own and with my talk therapist. It was discovered that as a child, the church members would have three-day, four-day, or even week-long fasts. No eating allowed. Nothing except water. You can imagine how hungry a child would get going without food. There is a gland in our brain that provides us with a chemical that releases and allows us to feel hungry. Mine was not working properly. Apparently, as a child, I had learned to suppress hunger to survive fasting, and it finally caught up with me in adulthood. I took a medication for a good six months until I felt comfortable without it. I was amazed the first time I felt hungry! What a unique feeling! Thankfully, I recovered my health and kept moving on in my journey of healing.

As I stated above, I kept myself in this little cocoon for a good three years or so. I had created a space of solitude and healing for myself and was loath to come out and do much socializing with family or friends.

It was Christmas 2001. I volunteered to work so my coworkers who had family, children, etc., could spend the holiday with their families. I went home from work on December 26, and for the first time in my life, as I sat journaling, I felt this intense loneliness. I had never experienced this feeling before, and I have to say this is not the most pleasant of feelings! In the past, I preferred to be alone because it was a way to protect myself from being hurt. I had always been comfortable being alone, and all of a sudden, I felt so intensely alone all I could do was cry. I felt all alone, and with this aloneness was a feeling of vulnerability. I felt confused by this feeling. Why now? It was the weekend, and I had two whole days to feel this before I could go back to work and be around people. That had to be the longest weekend in history!

A few months earlier (July), I had a coworker come to my office, waving a picture in front of me. It was a relative of hers she wanted me to meet. A man. "I want you to meet my uncle," she said. I immediately replied no. In no uncertain terms, "No, I do not want to meet your uncle." That was the last thing I needed right now. I had had enough. This coworker would show me this picture once in a while, but my answer was always no until that day in December 2001.

When I got to work after that long and lonely weekend, the first thing I did was page her to my office. I gave her my phone number and asked her to give it to her uncle. The poor man—when he called me, I wasn't really all that nice. I told him my "rules," and he agreed to meet me for coffee. In all honesty, I'm amazed he didn't just hang up on me. I look back on this now and see how silly I must have sounded to him, but he didn't shy away. Sometimes God really has a sense of humor because all I can say about this time in my life is *wow*. I was about to get the most awesome lesson about love, human nature, souls, and God all wrapped in one person. A person who was being put into my life to help me overcome my fear of God; my fear of the afterlife; my questions of whether there really was a God or not; and, most importantly, acceptance. This was my time to learn about letting go of negative control and trusting the process of life and living as we all know it.

LET GO AND LET GOD

Rodney and I met on December 28, 2001, in the parking lot of a McDonald's. He was a tall drink of refreshing water! Quite handsome with the most beautiful blue eyes I had ever seen. I actually felt nervous meeting him, which was quite unusual for me. When I tried to meet his gaze, I felt like he was trying to look inside my soul, and it made me uncomfortable. When he opened my car door to help me out, I looked up at him and felt an immediate connection somehow that I had never experienced before with anyone. I sensed immediately that this man was special. Even though I sensed this connection, I also felt a bit apprehensive. We went inside to grab some coffee and then sat down. Honestly, I couldn't tell you what we talked about. I know I talked to him while trying to make sense of the feelings that were swirling around inside my mind. I found it quite hard to look him in the eye. I think I was afraid he wouldn't like what he saw if I allowed him to look too deeply. When we left to go our separate ways, I wasn't sure I wanted to see him again. I felt scared and confused.

I went home with my mind wandering, trying to figure out what it was about this man that felt so different. I was concerned I was stepping into another situation that could be detrimental to me and my personal growth. I didn't want to take any more steps back, yet somehow, I sensed this man wouldn't hurt me or abuse me. I don't know why I knew this. I just did. I went to bed that night thinking about the meeting and our conversation. I watched him, and I could tell he felt this strange "connection" too, yet neither of us acknowledged it out loud. As I drifted off to sleep, I felt a smile on my face.

I had the most vivid dream that night. We all dream. We can dream in color or black and white. Some of us fly while we dream and awake with the sense of "What just happened to me?" In this dream, I could see two screens with two different scenarios, and I knew I had to choose. Both screens showed me love. Two different kinds of love. They were both unconditional love, but the feeling I got was that I could pick which one I wanted to experience. This dream was so intense that when I woke up, I had tears running down my face. With this dream so fresh in my mind, I knew I had to pick Rodney. I made the conscious decision to choose him and then waited for him to call.

Two long days passed with no call, and I was beginning to wonder if perhaps I had imagined this whole connection thing. I had little to no trust in myself or my gut and felt vulnerable in stepping out of the cocoon I had created within my apartment. The feelings I was experiencing were quite intense, and I felt a bit overwhelmed, but I *knew* I had to follow through if or when he called.

Finally, he called! We made arrangements to spend New Year's Eve together, and from that moment on, we were together every day until the day he passed away. For the first time in my life in a relationship, I felt only love. Just being in the same room was such a joy. What I failed to mention at the beginning of this story is that Rodney was battling cancer. When we met, he had already had one surgery and a round of chemo, and he thought he was well on his way to remission. I stepped into this relationship knowing about his illness and was fully ready to embrace the experience for the length of time we would have together. I knew I was taking the chance of losing him, but I chose to focus on the immediate moments we were spending together and not worry about the future.

Just two short months after we met, he had a recurrence of his cancer with a major surgery, chemo, and radiation; and I chose to be by his side happily. I realized I had to do this not because I loved him but because I also had been carrying around guilt for not being able to be with my dad for the last six months of his life. My relationship with my dad after his brain tumor surgery was painful for me, which caused me to not visit him often. I had always felt some guilt from this. I made the decision that I would be with Rodney no matter what. He tried to push me away, but I firmly argued that it was my choice and I was staying! Rodney knew I would be hurt when he passed away, but I was more than willing to go through the pain of loss for the pleasure of his company. You see, I looked at Rodney as a great gift in my life. During the three and a half years we spent together, we lived a lifetime. I was so amazed at the things we would talk about with each other. God, heaven, hell, the afterlife, and if there really was an afterlife. I believe he knew he was dying, although he never spoke the words out loud to me. We both cherished the time we spent together.

The closer he got to passing away, the deeper our conversations became. During this journey with him, when he was feeling anxious about death, we started praying together. My prayers were for him to feel peace, but in the back of my mind, I still had that nagging question of whether there really was a God and afterlife. I had no control over the health of this man I loved so much, and he was suffering as he continued to die such a slow, agonizing death. It was often gut-wrenching watching Rodney go through the difficult stages of his body shutting down so his soul could pass on to whatever came next.

There were many times he would ask me, "Do you think I'll go to hell? I've done so many things I'm not proud of. Why would God allow me to go to heaven when I have done things I shouldn't have?" I always told Rodney I *knew* he was going to heaven. In the back of my mind, though, I was just hoping there really was a God and a heaven!

Eventually, Rodney was placed in hospice. He began taking powerful medications to combat the pain and keep comfortable. It was amazing to me that he was still lucid and able to carry on conversations.

Around the three-week mark before his passing, we were having yet another conversation about heaven and God. Rodney had many visitors, but on this particular day, it was just him and me. We were enjoying a quiet afternoon for a change, and as I listened to him putting all the questions out into the room, I grabbed his hand and said, "Rodney, I need you to promise me something. Will you promise to try to do this for me after you pass, if it's at all possible?" He looked at me, and we both could feel the importance of what I was about to ask him. I presented two things to him and asked him for his promise to complete the tasks if it was at all possible after he passed. First, he needed to find my Skipper doggie and take care of him until I could get there. Second, he must give me a message so I would know without a doubt that he was still out there somewhere.

I had always been taught that animals have no soul, and this had always bothered me. I wanted proof that the animals we love so much had a place in heaven. After all, in my mind, heaven won't be heaven if my animals aren't there to be with me. All I knew about heaven was what I had heard from childhood and all the different scriptures written in the Bible, and I had doubts about everything I had been taught and exposed to as a child. I told Rodney to be sure and make the message hit me between the eyes, so to speak. I was so hardheaded, and I wanted to make sure I didn't miss it!

Rodney promised me if these things were possible, he would do his best to fulfill my requests. I knew in my heart he would do these things if it was possible. Three weeks later, after a long and difficult struggle, Rodney passed away. It was July 28, 2005. I was devastated. From the moment he passed, I felt a huge hole in my heart and an emptiness that no words can describe. I sat in my house with no tears. I was not able to even cry. It was the worst feeling I have ever felt in my life. My time spent with this man will forever be in my heart and mind, and I have no regrets. The whole experience with him was precious. I didn't realize it at the time, but during our time together, I learned to pray again.

I felt so empty. After the funeral services, as I struggled to function with work and everyday life, I began paying attention to everything around me, hoping I would receive a message from him. With each passing day, nothing happened. There were no messages. I was beginning to lose hope about the afterlife, God, and anything else related to religion and spiritual beliefs.

A week or so after losing Rodney, I began experiencing heart palpitations. I was at work one day and was wearing a heart monitor. I hid the wires as best as I could, but a lady came into the office and noticed the wires. She didn't know me as we had never met before. She conducted her business with my boss; and just as she was leaving, she stepped into my office, looked at me, and said, "You need to see a friend of mine. He is an intuitive, and I feel you need to see him." I didn't know what to say. I had always been taught that things like this were of the devil; and frankly, I just wasn't sure I believed in people who could see the future or talk to passed loved ones. She told me he was so popular that he had a wait list, so I figured there was little chance he would see me. She left, and I figured that was the end of that. I have to admit I was curious about her friend.

Within a few days, I received a call from this lady who informed me I had an appointment to see this intuitive. I looked him up online and discovered that he was well-known in our area and had helped many people over the years. He had also worked with the police, helping to locate missing persons. My curiosity was aroused, and I agreed to go visit him.

I'm not sure what I was expecting. When we arrived at his office, it was at the bottom of his home. The grounds were beautiful. As I got out of the car, I felt peacefulness in the air around me. I entered the waiting room and felt that peace settle over me. I had to wait a few minutes for my turn and was totally surprised when I stood up to meet this man. He had a calming presence about him, and even though I was nervous, he never once made me feel uncomfortable. I was thankful he looked so ordinary! You see all this crazy stuff on media and TV, and I wasn't sure what to expect! We sat down—he behind his desk, me in a comfortable armchair in front of the desk. I had all these thoughts about God and how mad He would be at me for indulging my curiosity, but I had come too far to run away from what was about to happen.

Mr. McGhee looked at me and smiled as he said, "So I see your significant other recently passed away. You know you and he had a special soul bond?" I was speechless. This man had never met me and knew nothing about me or my circumstances. How on earth could he have known about Rodney? I sat up straighter in the chair. He had my attention!

Aaron said, "Rodney wants me to tell you that you were the light of his life. He is standing with a dog and wants me to tell you that he's got him and loves him and will take care of him until you get there."

I began to openly sob. Here was my message from Rodney I had asked for before he died. I had been waiting for this! Emotions were flooding through me and all around me. Rodney was alive and really out there somewhere! There really is a place we go to when we die! The relief I felt was so intense and overwhelming! Aaron explained the connection we had, which helped me understand so many things. I knew by the time I left the appointment that Rodney was put in my life for a reason. Everything I experienced during our relationship was a great gift! By the time I left that appointment, I didn't care if I got punished by God.

It was worth any punishment to receive affirmation that there really is an afterlife, and it's not hellfire and brimstone!

As I got into the car for the drive home, I suddenly realized what the date was. It was August 28—Rodney's birthday! Coincidence? I think not! After my visit with Aaron, I was finally able to start my grieving process. The tears began to fall over my loss. It began as small waves, and at times, the grief would totally engulf me. I continued to watch for signs and messages as I grieved for the loss of part of my soul.

A month or so later, I had another vivid dream. Rodney came to me. He looked haggard and unshaven. He was leaning against the doorjamb of the bathroom, and I angrily asked him about my message. He replied that he was busy rejoicing with the Lord and healing from living on earth. He then told me to be patient and that he would come to me. I woke up the next morning feeling perplexed. I thought I had already received my message! I put away the dream from my mind and headed off to work.

As December approached, I began feeling a dread of the upcoming holidays. This would be my first holiday season without Rodney, and I was not looking forward to this experience. I bought a new TV and put it in my bedroom so I could sit up in bed, eat, and watch TV. I liked having it on for the noise. It was a few days before Christmas. When I settled in to eat my dinner and watch TV, I ate and immediately got so sleepy! This was unusual for me. I was a true night owl. I would often read or watch TV until quite late before finally drifting off to sleep. This particular night, I felt so sleepy I decided to snuggle in early. I turned off the TV and lamp and was settling under the covers. I glanced at the clock. It said 9:26 p.m. I remember thinking how odd it was that I felt so sleepy but closed my eyes anyway to slip off into dreamland.

What happened next I can only describe as the most profound spiritual experience of my life. Just a few moments after settling the covers around me, I felt a strange vibration. At first, I thought the bed was vibrating. I turned over and resettled the covers, thinking that I had myself in a bind with the sheets; but then I noticed that the bed was still vibrating. I opened my eyes to look at the wall above me to see if the shadow of the bedpost was shaking on the wall. It wasn't. I then realized that it wasn't the bed vibrating. It was my body. It felt like a gentle shaking or vibrating. I instantly felt fear.

All sorts of questions began racing through my mind. Was I getting ready to have a heart attack? Was I having a stroke? I aimed my focus at my heart and realized that I wasn't feeling any pain, so it must not be my heart. I felt my fear begin to subside. As the fear left, I instantly felt a heat in my body that started at my lower back and quickly spread out to all parts of my body. It was a pleasant sensation, and by this time, I had the thought, "Am I having a spiritual experience?" I began feeling the vibration become stronger. I opened my eyes briefly, but all I could see were colorful lines. I immediately closed my eyes again and allowed all my fear to leave. At that moment, instantaneously, I sensed something standing in the room at the foot of my bed. Even though I had my eyes closed, I could see a presence standing there, and I felt wonder and awe because I *knew* it was God. He was standing right there! I say *He*, but in all honesty, it didn't look like any sex or human being. It was just this wonderful presence of energy, and I knew it was God. I felt this energy say hello to me, and then it came close to me as I lay there. I began to experience a feeling so overwhelming that the energy had to move back again because I couldn't handle the proximity.

I also felt Rodney within this presence and realized that this presence had brought Rodney to me for my message. The feeling I got was that Rodney and this energy (God) were one and the same. It was amazing to feel this realization! Once this energy knew I understood what was happening, Rodney emerged from the presence and came to my bedside. He wasn't sick anymore and asked my permission to "join" with me. I felt and understood what he meant and agreed immediately.

As he joined me, I felt my body lying in the bed. I could feel the weight of my body, but I was having such an amazing experience that I just had no care about my body lying there. The spirit of Rodney climbed over me, and we "spooned" in the bed, lying there and enjoying being with each other again. I felt him wrap his arms around me. The feelings of joy were amazing! I had so many questions! As all the questions formed in my mind, they were answered as quickly as I could think of each one. I recognized that I wasn't talking out loud. The whole conversation was done in our minds and felt in the body.

One of my requests was to show me where he was. As the thought came to my mind, I felt myself rising. Suddenly, Rodney and I were walking side by side, and he was showing me where he was. It was quite beautiful. The colors were more pronounced somehow, and the lighting (like sunlight) was different. I could feel myself absorbing the light as we walked around, almost like I was using the light to feed myself. I saw lots of other people or beings during this tour but didn't speak to any of them. Rodney shared his new world with me, and it was beautiful!

Just as suddenly as I was up and walking around, I became aware of my body. I could feel the heaviness of my body lying in the bed like a dead weight. Rodney helped me climb back into my body and told me it was time to go. I didn't argue with him. I could somehow "feel" that our visit was coming to an end. As we lay there hugging and spooning for the last time, I felt Rodney begin to rise and pull away. Right before he left completely, I felt something warm come into my heart and fill an empty space inside. It was a feeling that he was giving me something to help me live the rest of my life without having to bear that horrible emptiness I had been feeling in my heart.

As I sensed him leaving, the warmth at the beginning of this whole experience began to slowly ebb back to the small of my back and then ease away. The vibrations left as quietly as the warmth, and I realized I was in my bedroom again and awake.

I opened my eyes and noticed the peace and quiet all around me. I sat up on the side of the bed and immediately pinched myself on the arm to see if I felt any pain. I felt the need to make sure I was awake and not dreaming. I glanced at my clock and saw the time was 12:36 a.m.

As I sat there trying to wrap my head around what had just happened, I realized that what had felt like only moments had lasted exactly three hours! I pinched my arm again to make sure I was awake. I pinched myself again—it hurt! I knew I was awake. I got up and wandered around the house. What had just happened to me? I got to meet God! Rodney came and gave me my message, and I had no doubt that was what had just happened!

The feelings I felt—elation, relief, happiness, sadness, awe—were on so many levels that the English language sadly cannot describe! All my questions had been answered. There really is a God. There is an afterlife.

I saw animals in the place Rodney showed me! We really do have a soul or essence that is reunited with a higher power after we shed this body and die!

I didn't sleep for three days after this experience. I didn't feel the need for sleep. The amazing thing about this experience is that it was so personal. I figured no one would ever know anything had happened unless I told them. Frankly, I figured I would be looked at as crazy if I told anyone about my experience. However, I discovered quickly that people do notice. I got to work the next morning, and all day long, my coworkers asked me if I had done something new with my hair or makeup. They kept stopping at my office door and telling me something was different about me. The only explanation I had was this experience of my "visit" from God and Rodney. I smiled for three days as I processed the whole experience in my mind.

In the years since this happened to me, I have come to the realization that lots of people have these spiritual experiences, but they choose not to share the details for fear of being labeled crazy. In my opinion, that's a darn shame! All I know is the visit I received from God and Rodney has helped me in numerous ways for the last eighteen years and given me the reassurance I needed that there is a loving being looking over us. We are not alone by any means. I believe we have a lot to look forward to when we reach the end of our lives. Death is just the beginning!

The valuable lesson from this whole experience is that our soul is our essence; it is our individual piece of God that is with us always. It is part of who we are as human beings. Our soul is our "truth." With this newfound information, why do I still feel fear when I think about God?

THE FEAR FACTOR

I don't remember exactly when I first realized I was scared of God. I just knew that I was. Once this reality became clear in my mind, I began to take a look at my personal belief system. I began to see that many of the choices I made in life were made with the underlying thought and the worry that God would be unhappy with my choices. For example, each morning, when I woke up, I always mentally said a quick hello to God before my day began. I did this because I had this small worry that if I

CHRISTINE PETERS

didn't, I was being a bad person. Silly, isn't it? Such a simple small thing this greeting was, but to me, it was a big deal. I feared punishment from God if I didn't greet Him each morning.

To understand my fear of God better, I decided it was time to take a deep, long, hard look at what I had been taught as a child about God. I wanted to go over every single lesson, thought, and comment I had ever heard and try to figure out where all this fear was coming from. It took me some time to do this as my childhood had been quite difficult.

I feel being exposed to so much hellfire-and-brimstone preaching contributed to much of my fear, along with different things I picked up from TV, literature, and just people in general. I always took everything at face value and believed everything I was told. I would sit down and look up all the scriptures in the Bible about God being angry. I slowly began to realize that because I was so young, I had absorbed so much negativity about God that everything I thought about God was a skewed mess!

I look back over my life experiences and realize that God had nothing to do with all the misery. Everything I thought I knew had been taught to me by men. Human beings who are not perfect. One of the most damaging things I was taught is that God is up in heaven, not in me. I was taught that God is outside and apart from me. I thought I always had to look up to God to hear me when I prayed. The absolute worst part of my fear was thinking that all the hardships—my dad being sick and my being molested—were entirely my fault. It was no wonder I had such fear with all this nonsense being drilled into my head as a child!

As horrible as all this childhood reality sounds, after many years of counseling and looking within, I finally began to ask myself the hard questions and read books to educate myself to a better understanding of God.

I am happy to report that with a lot of work, tears, hardships, etc., I have finally figured out that all my fears were man-made. I had done nothing wrong to deserve all the hardships. Now, if I can heal from all this fear, so can you!

CHAPTER 7

WHO AND WHAT DO YOU REALLY TRUST?

Finding peace in life is all about being who you are meant to be before all the outside influences around you can lead you down any road of negative emotions. As children, from the moment we begin having memories of our lives, we get exposed to many different things and lessons that can color who we become as we continue to age. Teaching our children about their feelings and how to use them effectively, I believe, is the key to a healthy, balanced, meaningful life. We are all created with feelings, which begin to work from the moment we are born. A baby will cry when it is hungry, wet, or has an upset tummy, for example.

When a child expresses emotion as a baby, we are quick to pay attention and fix whatever is causing them to cry, and they settle into sleep or smile up at us. Unfortunately, as the child grows older, we have a tendency to begin to teach them to ignore their feelings with comments like "Don't cry" or "Hush now. Big boys don't cry." We begin teaching them at an early age to not express their feelings. In extreme cases, this can cause terrible damage to their thought processes as they continue to get older. As children are exposed to more and more outside influences, they are taught more and more to ignore their feelings or not pay attention to them.

All through my deprogramming and healing process, I began to notice a pattern. The whole process was about acknowledging my personal feelings and then allowing myself to feel the feelings so I could heal and move on. To feel the feelings, I had to understand the *why* part of the feelings. Once I realized the *why* of the feelings, I was able to feel them, process them, heal them, soothe myself, and move on to the next one.

I have learned that trust is a big feeling. Too many times, we allow ourselves to trust someone for one reason or another and later discover that perhaps we should have held some of that trust back because they betrayed us. Instead of trusting immediately, we find it healthier to build the trust again. Looking back, you could probably see the red flags flying but chose to ignore them. Why did you ignore them? Have you ever asked yourself that question? I believe we choose to ignore the red flags because there is something lacking in ourselves. For me, I was so hungry for unconditional love that I would fall right into a horrible situation with no thought to question anything! On top of that, I was not taught to question my feelings. In all honesty, I learned at an early age to squash any feelings I had and go by the feelings of others.

Ultimately, I have learned to pay attention to my body's reactions or any feelings that arise within myself, and I now question everything if something feels off. To question is to begin the process of trust within yourself. Being honest with yourself builds your inner trust, which leads to a better, healthier, more balanced life.

Trusting yourself is a "built-in" guidepost to help us make better decisions for ourselves. I believe God created us with feelings so we would have this built-in system to help us live our lives easier. Our feelings also tie in with our "gut" or intuition. For me, trusting myself, much less trusting God, wasn't even a glimmer on my radar for years! It felt as if my "system" was broken! I would ask myself why I should trust a God who is so full of judgment and anger toward me. How does one trust a God who hands out punishment like candy?

The first step for me was understanding that it is OK to feel my feelings and OK to trust myself. I wish I could tell you that trusting my feelings came to me quickly, but it did not. For quite a while, I was still looking over my shoulder, waiting for God to punish me somehow for paying attention to my feelings!

I finally came to realize that God created me with feelings. My feelings are part of my soul. My soul is part of God. Therefore, God is within me. He has been my whole life! By trusting my feelings (that God gave me), I am also trusting God. God speaks to us through our feelings. Feelings never steer you wrong and are always with you!

So who do you trust? You, of course! By trusting yourself, you are honoring and trusting God.

CHAPTER 8

MAKING THE CONNECTION

I wish to make this very clear. I write this book not because I am a victim but because I consider myself to be a victor! Like that old hymn "Victory Is Mine." Once I finally made that connection that God was within me and always had been, I began shedding all the weight of the spiritual abuse I experienced as a child. Our religions are teaching us that we must pray and be saved by God to go to heaven. This is just not true! God is in each and every one of us because He created us that way! Instead of looking all around you to find some peace, look within! Your peace is there, waiting for you to acknowledge it! As a dear friend once said to me, "It is hell to be happy and easy to be sad." The reason it is hell to be happy is that we are all so conditioned (by religion, by society, by family, and by friends) to look outside of ourselves when we should really be looking within!

Looking within is not easy. You have to be willing to take a look at all the "ugly truth" and choices you have made in life. You have to be willing to really get to know yourself inside and out. So many times, the outer person we present to the public is very different from the inner person.

Know and understand this when all else fails. Use this thought to comfort you: we all come from God. We all have God within us. We are born on this earth with God in us. If you can trust yourself, you trust God.

LISTEN TO THE SONG OF YOUR SOUL

Now that you realize God is trustworthy, believe it and know it. Allow yourself to feel the "knowingness" in your heart and go out and live life with joyful freedom. The possibilities are limitless! I continue to learn new things each day, and I am open to learning any lessons that might come my way.

I cannot express enough the importance of acknowledging your feelings. These feelings are the songs of your soul! When you become aware of your feelings and acknowledge them, you are not only honoring yourself but are also honoring God within you!

I want to issue a challenge to you as you read this final chapter. If you are attending a church and feel any negative emotions at all, run. Leave and ask yourself why you feel something negative. Has something been preached about that doesn't sit right with you? Are you feeling conflicted about a sermon that just doesn't feel right? Are there some unusual rules in your church that prohibit you from worshipping fully? Are there any functions you are not allowed to participate in because of church policy? Does the church you attend lead you to believe their denomination is the right one and the only one that will get you to heaven? If you answer yes to any of these questions, then for goodness' sake, *leave*! Don't walk! Run!

God is not about anything negative! He is all about love and everything positive. Give yourself permission to hear your inner voice. If you have children, pay attention to any words they might say after being in this religious atmosphere. Young children are much more open to their inner feelings than we are as adults. Young children have an easier time speaking the truth when they are not punished!

Remember, God doesn't punish! He, however, allows us to experience the consequences of our actions. This is our free will—yet another wonderful thing we are created with upon birth!

Once you allow yourself to look within and explore your core beliefs of what you think and feel about God, you may find that life becomes more joyful, and the feeling of freedom is sublime.

Be joyful, my friends, and may your journey of self-discovery and healing bring you the joy of fulfillment and heaven on earth!

ABOUT THE AUTHOR

Christine Peters is just one of the many beautiful souls who happen to be spending a life here on the planet we call Earth. She lives her life simply with her husband and dogs and, in her spare time, writes books about her personal experiences and lessons she has learned. She knew from an early age that she had a connection with flowers, so she became a floral designer, working her way into owning a floral shop and, in later years, becoming a freelance floral designer traveling around the States.

For years, her friends and colleagues encouraged her to write as her life experiences and stories she shared seemed to touch the lives of those around her. Presently, Christine is enjoying time off from the hustle and bustle of the busy world we live in while puttering around out in the yard, digging flower beds happily as ideas pop into her mind about future books!

Printed in the United States
by Baker & Taylor Publisher Services